TOKYO DISNEY RESORT VACATION GUIDE 2025

Discover the Magic of TOKYO DISNEY RESORT, Explore Disneyland, Disney Sea, Attractions, Dining, Hidden Gems, Tips, Itineraries, and Exclusive Experiences for Families, Couples, and Solo Travelers

GEORGE RICHARD

All rights reserved. No part of this publication may be reproduced, distributed, or transmitted in any form or by any means, including photocopying, recording, or other electronic or mechanical methods, without the prior written permission of the publisher, except in the case of brief quotations embodied in critical reviews and certain other noncommercial uses permitted by copyright law.

Copyright © George Richard, 2025.

Table of Contents

Introduction **10**
   Why Visit Tokyo Disney Resort in 2025? 11
   Tips for First-Timers at Tokyo Disney Resort 13

Planning Your Trip **18**
   Best Time to Visit 18
      Seasons and Weather 18
      Special Seasonal Events and Festivals 20
   How to Get There 23
      From Tokyo Airports to the Resort 23
      Transportation Around Tokyo Disney Resort 25
   Accommodation Options Near Tokyo Disney Resort... 26
      Disney Hotels and Resorts 26
      Nearby Hotels for Every Budget 29
      Best Family-Friendly, Couple-Friendly, and Solo Traveler Hotels 31
   Budgeting Your Trip 32
      Estimated Costs (Tickets, Food, Souvenirs, etc.) 33
      Money-Saving Tips for a Disney Vacation 35
      Special Offers and Deals 36

Attractions **38**
   Tokyo Disneyland 38
      Must-See Attractions 38
      Top Rides for Families, Couples, and Solo Travelers 40

Iconic Shows and Parades 42

Seasonal and Special Attractions for 2025 43

Tokyo DisneySea 43

Overview of DisneySea's Themed Lands 44

Best Rides and Attractions at DisneySea 45

Exclusive Shows and Events at DisneySea 47

Attractions by Age Group 47

Best Attractions for Young Kids 47

Teen-Friendly and Thrill-Seeking Rides 50

Fun for Adults and Seniors 52

Top Attractions for Families, Couples, and Solo Travelers 55

Dining 57

Best Restaurants for Families, Couples, and Solo Travelers 57

Character Dining Experiences 57

Themed Restaurants 59

Quick Service vs. Fine Dining 62

Dining Plans and Reservations 64

How to Make Dining Reservations 64

Disney Dining Plans (If Available) 65

Hidden Dining Gems 66

Off-the-Beaten-Path Restaurants 66

Unique and Secret Dining Experiences 70

Must-Try Dishes at Tokyo Disney Resort 71

Shopping and Souvenirs 74

Where to Shop for Disney Merchandise 74
    Exclusive Disney Products 74
    Must-Buy Souvenirs and Gifts 76
What to Buy for Families, Couples, and Solo Travelers 79
    Personalized Gifts and Memorabilia 79
    Best Souvenirs for Each Type of Visitor 80
Hidden Shopping Spots 82
    Lesser-Known Shops for Unique Finds 82
    Secret Souvenirs Only Disney Fans Will Know 83

Hidden Gems and Lesser-Known Spots 85
Secret Areas to Explore 85
    Quiet Spots for Relaxing and Photos 85
    Hidden-Themed Areas You May Miss 88
Underrated Attractions 90
Off-the-Beaten-Path Experiences 92

Exclusive Experiences 95
VIP Tours and Special Access 95
    How to Book VIP Tours and Behind-the-Scenes Experiences 95
    Exclusive Access to Rides, Shows, and Events 98
Character Meet-and-Greets 99
    Best Times and Locations to Meet Your Favorite Characters 99
    Rare and Exclusive Character Appearances 101
Seasonal Events and Festivals in 2025 102

Limited-Time Events and Shows at Tokyo Disney Resort 102

Itineraries.. 105

1-Day Itinerary for Families, Couples, and Solo Travelers 105

A Perfect Day for Families 105

A Romantic Day for Couples 107

Solo Traveler's Guide to Tokyo Disney Resort 110

Multiple-Day Itinerary 112

3-Day Itinerary: Making the Most of Your Time.... 112

5-Day Itinerary: Exploring Every Corner of the Resort 114

7-Day Itinerary: Extended Stay with Day Trips 115

Rides and Shows to Prioritize 116

Which Attractions You Can't Miss 116

Tips and Tricks for a Magical Experience 117

Maximizing Your Time.. 117

Using the Tokyo Disney Resort App....................... 117

Best Strategies for Beating the Lines 118

FastPass and Queue Management Tips 120

Dealing with Crowds.. 121

When to Visit Specific Attractions to Avoid the Crowds 121

Off-Peak Hours for Maximum Enjoyment............. 122

Packing Essentials 123

What to Bring and What to Leave Behind 124

7 |TOKYO DISNEY RESORT

Weather-Appropriate Packing Tips 125
Language and Cultural Tips 126
    Basic Japanese Phrases to Know 127
    Understanding Japanese Customs and Etiquette 128
Tech Tips 130
    Best Apps for Tokyo Disney Resort 130
    Using Mobile Payments and Other Tech Solutions for Convenience 133

Seasonal Events and Parades 135

Holiday Celebrations 135
    Special Events During Christmas, New Year's, and Halloween 136
Must-See Parades, Shows, and Fireworks 139
    Best Times to Catch Parades and Fireworks 139
    Where to Sit for the Best Views 140
Themed Events and Festivals in 2025 141
    Special 2025-Only Events You Shouldn't Miss 141

Beyond the Parks 144

Exploring Tokyo Beyond Disney 144
    Must-See Attractions in Tokyo: Shrines, Museums, and Shopping 145
    Top Cultural Experiences in the City 149
Day Trips from Tokyo Disney Resort 151
    Visiting Mount Fuji 152
    Kyoto: The Cultural Capital of Japan 153
    Other Iconic Locations in Japan 154

Safety and Accessibility **155**
   Health and Safety Guidelines.. 155
      COVID-19 Updates and Travel Precautions 155
      Other Health and Safety Tips 157
   Accessible Travel Tips.. 158
      Services for Guests with Disabilities....................... 158
      Mobility Assistance and Special Needs Information 161
   Childcare and Family Services... 162
      Baby Care Stations and Family-Friendly Services.. 163

Conclusion **165**
   Making the Most of Your Magical Trip..................... 165
   Final Words of Inspiration 171

Bonus Content **173**
   Packing List for Tokyo Disney Resort....................... 173

FAQs.. **178**

Photo section.. **187**

Introduction

Welcome to one of the world's most enchanting and thrilling destinations—Tokyo Disney Resort! Nestled in the heart of Japan, this magical wonderland is the ultimate escape for families, couples, and solo adventurers alike. Whether you're a Disney enthusiast or just looking for a once-in-a-lifetime experience, Tokyo Disney Resort offers everything you need to create memories that will last forever.

As a seasoned traveler, I've had the pleasure of visiting many theme parks across the globe, but there's something uniquely captivating about Tokyo Disney Resort that sets it apart. From the cutting-edge attractions at DisneySea to the classic Disney magic at Disneyland, this Resort seamlessly combines innovative entertainment, impeccable hospitality, and a touch of Disney's beloved nostalgia. This guide will help you navigate everything the Resort offers so you can make the most of your trip.

Tokyo Disney Resort comprises two main parks: **Tokyo Disneyland** and **Tokyo DisneySea.** In addition to these, you'll find luxurious hotels, shopping areas, fine dining, and themed experiences that go above and beyond your expectations. Whether you're here for one day or an entire week, you'll never run out of things to do, see, and enjoy.

This is your gateway to a magical adventure, and I'm here to ensure that you have the best possible experience.

Why Visit Tokyo Disney Resort in 2025?

So, why is 2025 the perfect year to visit Tokyo Disney Resort? Here's why this year is one of the most exciting times to experience the magic of Disney:

1. **New Attractions and Updates**

In 2025, you'll find many new attractions and updates that will take your experience to the next level. Disney is constantly innovating and improving, and 2025 is no exception. Whether you're a fan of thrilling rides or immersive, state-of-the-art experiences, there's something fresh to discover.

2. **The Resort's 40th Anniversary Celebration**

Tokyo Disneyland is celebrating its **40th Anniversary** in 2025, marking a monumental milestone. Special events, limited-time parades, exclusive merchandise, and themed attractions will be available to mark this historic occasion. It's the perfect time to visit for fans of Disney nostalgia and those who want to be part of the celebration.

3. **Seasonal and Themed Events**

Tokyo Disney Resort is known for its exceptional seasonal events, from Halloween to Christmas. In 2025, expect more immersive experiences with new seasonal parades, themed rides, and limited-time dining options. The 2025 season promises to be full of Disney-themed magic that changes throughout the year. With these unique additions, you'll experience the Resort like never before.

4. New Dining Experiences

Disney's dining offerings have been continuously evolving, and in 2025, there will be new restaurants, character dining experiences, and exclusive dishes that will delight your taste buds and your Instagram feed. Whether you're craving a quick snack or a fine dining experience, there's always something new to discover in the culinary world of Tokyo Disney Resort.

5. Improved Technology and Park Features

Tokyo Disney Resort embraces the latest technology to make your visit smoother and more enjoyable. From mobile apps that help you navigate the parks to enhanced virtual queue systems for popular attractions, you'll notice an increased emphasis on tech-savvy experiences that make it easier to plan your day. Plus, expect more innovative Disney magic throughout the park as technology continues to enhance the immersive experience.

6. Exclusive Merchandise

Whether you're a collector or just looking for a unique souvenir, 2025 will bring a range of **exclusive anniversary merchandise** that celebrates Tokyo Disney Resort's history and future. You won't miss these unique collectibles available during this special year.

In short, 2025 is the year to be at Tokyo Disney Resort. With fresh experiences, exciting anniversaries, and innovative updates, there's no better time to immerse yourself in Disney magic.

Tips for First-Timers at Tokyo Disney Resort

If you've never visited Tokyo Disney Resort before, don't worry—this section will guide you through everything you need to know to make your first visit seamless and unforgettable. Here are some practical tips to ensure you have the best experience possible:

1. Plan Your Trip Well in Advance

Tokyo Disney Resort is a popular destination, so planning your visit ahead of time is essential. Start by booking your hotel, tickets, and dining reservations as early as possible. This is particularly important during peak seasons such as holidays, weekends, and anniversaries like the **40th Anniversary** in 2025 when the Resort can get quite crowded.

- **Buy Your Tickets Online**: To save time and avoid long queues, purchase your tickets online. You can select between single-day tickets or multi-day passes depending on your stay. Be sure to check for any special ticket offers or discounts that may be available in 2025.

- **Make Dining Reservations Early**: If you want to dine at one of the Resort's popular restaurants, especially character dining locations, make reservations as soon as possible. Popular spots fill up quickly, and you don't want to miss out on the unique dining experiences at Tokyo Disney Resort.

2. Know the Parks and Plan Your Itinerary

Tokyo Disney Resort has two main parks: **Tokyo Disneyland** and **Tokyo DisneySea**. Both parks offer a completely different experience, so it's key to plan which park to visit each day.

- **Tokyo Disneyland**: This park is filled with classic Disney charm, from iconic rides like *Pirates of the Caribbean* to parades and shows that make you feel like you've stepped into a Disney movie.

- **Tokyo DisneySea**: A one-of-a-kind park that blends Disney magic with nautical themes. It's ideal for fans of immersive experiences, and it offers some of the best attractions Disney has to offer, including *Journey to the Center of the Earth* and *Tower of Terror*.

- **Tip**: If you only have one day, you should focus on one park to avoid feeling rushed. However, if you have multiple days, I recommend spending one day in each park to get the whole experience.

3. Arrive Early to Beat the Crowds

- One of the best tips for first-timers is to arrive **early**. Tokyo Disney Resort opens its gates promptly, and if you get there as the park opens, you can beat the rush and enjoy popular attractions with shorter wait times.

- **FastPass and Virtual Queues**: Utilize the **FastPass** system to skip long lines for select attractions. Using the Resort's app, you can reserve times for popular rides like *Splash Mountain* and *Big Thunder Mountain*, so you don't have to wait. Tokyo Disney Resort also offers virtual queues for some of the newest or most popular attractions, so be sure to check the app for real-time updates on how to join them.

4. Be Prepared for the Weather

Tokyo has four distinct seasons, and the Weather can vary significantly depending on when you visit. Be sure to check the weather forecast before your trip and pack accordingly.

- **Summer (June - August)**: Tokyo can get very hot and humid, so wear lightweight clothing, bring sunscreen, and drink plenty of water. Many attractions have indoor waiting areas with air conditioning, but the outdoor queues can be challenging during peak summer.

- **Winter (December - February)**: If you're visiting in winter, expect cooler temperatures, especially in the evenings. Bring a warm jacket, as temperatures can drop significantly after dark.

- **Spring and Autumn** are the most pleasant seasons, with mild temperatures and beautiful seasonal changes. They're also the best times to experience the seasonal events at the park, like cherry blossoms in spring or autumn foliage.

5. Download the Tokyo Disney Resort App

- The **Tokyo Disney Resort App** is your best friend for navigating the parks. The app provides up-to-date information on wait times, available FastPasses, restaurant reservations, showtimes, and park maps.

- **Tip**: Use the app to plan your day, track wait times, and locate your favorite attractions. You can also check out real-time updates on parades, character meet-and-greets, and any last-minute changes to show schedules.

6. Stay Hydrated and Take Breaks

- Visiting Tokyo Disney Resort can be physically demanding, with many walking and standing in lines. Make sure to stay hydrated throughout the day. There are water refill stations throughout the parks, and you can also find cold drinks at most food carts and restaurants.

- **Tip**: Take breaks when you need them, and don't hesitate to visit some of the quieter spots in the park to recharge.

7. Make the Most of Parades and Shows

- Tokyo Disney Resort is famous for its **parades and live shows**. These are not to be missed, especially during the seasonal events or the 40th Anniversary celebrations in 2025.

- **Tip**: Check the schedule for parades, fireworks, and stage shows early in the day, so you can plan accordingly. Arriving early will help you get a good viewing spot, especially for the nightly fireworks displays.

8. Be Ready for the Disney Magic

- Lastly, remember to **embrace the magic of Disney**. Whether it's a thrilling ride, a meeting with your favorite Disney character, or simply strolling through the beautifully themed areas, Tokyo Disney Resort is all about creating unforgettable memories.

- **Tip**: Don't forget to take photos! The entire Resort is a photographer's dream, with iconic backdrops, gorgeous landscapes, and moments of Disney magic that you'll want to capture.

Planning Your Trip

Best Time to Visit

When planning your trip to Tokyo Disney Resort, consider the best time to visit based on the Weather, crowd levels, and special events throughout the year. Here, I'll provide you with everything you need to know to choose the right time for your visit.

Seasons and Weather

Tokyo has four seasons, each offering a different experience at Tokyo Disney Resort. Here's a breakdown of what to expect for each season:

1. **Spring (March to May)**
    - **Weather**: Temperatures range from **10°C to 20°C (50°F to 68°F)**, with mild days and cool evenings.
    - **What to Expect**: Spring is one of the most pleasant times to visit Tokyo Disney Resort. The Weather is comfortable for walking around the parks, and you can experience the beauty of cherry blossoms in late March or early April.
    - **Tip**: Be sure to pack light layers. A jacket is helpful for the cooler evenings, but you can usually get away with a T-shirt during the day.

2. **Summer (June to August)**
   - **Weather**: It is hot and humid, with temperatures ranging from **25°C to 35°C (77°F to 95°F)** and high humidity.
   - **What to Expect**: Summer is the busiest time at Tokyo Disney Resort, especially during school vacation. It's the perfect time for water-themed attractions and enjoying the fireworks shows, but be prepared for long lines and crowded parks.
   - **Tip**: Dress in lightweight, moisture-wicking clothing to stay comfortable. Bring sunscreen and sunglasses, and stay hydrated. Summer also sees afternoon rain, so carrying a small, foldable umbrella is a good idea.

3. **Autumn (September to November)**
   - **Weather**: Temperatures range from **15°C to 25°C (59°F to 77°F)**, with lower humidity and cooler evenings. This is the most comfortable Weather for park-goers.
   - **What to Expect**: Autumn is another great time to visit Tokyo Disney Resort. The fall foliage provides beautiful backdrops for photos, and the parks aren't as crowded as in summer. The Weather is perfect for spending the whole day outdoors.

- **Tip**: Pack a light jacket for the evening, as temperatures can drop, but you won't need heavy winter wear.

4. **Winter (December to February)**
   - **Weather**: Temperatures range from **5°C to 10°C (41°F to 50°F)**. It's chilly but rarely too cold to walk around the parks. Snowfall is rare but can occur in January.
   - **What to Expect**: Tokyo Disney Resort looks magical during the winter months, with holiday decorations, themed events, and chilly nights. The crowds tend to be lighter in December (after the New Year) and January, making it ideal for avoiding long wait times.
   - **Tip**: Bring a warm coat, scarf, and gloves. If you visit during the holiday season, expect festive parades and special events.

Special Seasonal Events and Festivals

One of the best things about Tokyo Disney Resort is the incredible **seasonal events** and **festivals** that change annually. These events often feature exclusive parades, merchandise, food, and performances, giving visitors a unique experience each time they visit. Here are some key events to keep in mind for your 2025 trip:

1. **Spring (March to May)**
   - **Spring Celebration**: This event celebrates the blooming of the cherry blossoms. Expect special themed parades, photo opportunities, and exclusive spring-time merchandise.
   - **Easter**: From late March to mid-April, you'll find Easter-themed decorations, snacks, and character meet-and-greets with bunny-themed outfits.
   - **Flower Festival**: In DisneySea, the spring season brings a floral festival, during which gardens and areas are decorated with vibrant flowers.

2. **Summer (June to August)**
   - **Disney Summer Festival**: A fun-filled summer event featuring special parades, water-based attractions, and limited-edition summer-themed snacks. Don't miss the spectacular **fireworks shows** at night, which highlight the summer experience.
   - **Tanabata (Star Festival)**: Celebrated in July, Tanabata is a Japanese festival based on a legend of star-crossed lovers. The Resort offers special events, lanterns, and decorations during this time.
   - **Splash Summer Fun**: Water-themed events at the parks are a perfect way to

beat the heat, with water-related rides, splash zones, and special water-themed shows.

3. **Autumn (September to November)**
   - **Halloween**: From late September through October, the parks are transformed with Halloween decorations, spooky parades, and Halloween-themed food. Expect special Halloween merchandise and character meet-and-greets with Disney villains.
   - **Autumn Festival**: In DisneySea, enjoy beautiful autumn foliage, seasonal food offerings, and special performances celebrating the fall season.
   - **Thanksgiving**: Although not as big as Halloween, Tokyo Disney Resort often celebrates Thanksgiving with special meals and themed treats in November.

4. **Winter (December to February)**
   - **Christmas**: Tokyo Disney Resort is particularly magical during the Christmas season (mid-November to December). The parks are decorated with beautiful Christmas trees, lights, and festive shows. Holiday-themed merchandise and limited-edition treats are in abundance.
   - **New Year's Eve and Day**: The Resort hosts special New Year's Eve events, such

as the **New Year's Eve Countdown Party**, which features parades, shows, and fireworks. New Year's Day is marked by limited-time food offerings and Disney-themed traditions.

- **Winter Wonderland**: The park creates a winter wonderland feel with light displays, holiday parades, and cozy indoor spots for visitors to warm up. Many restaurants have a special winter menu, perfect for enjoying a hot meal after a day at the park.

How to Get There

Once you've decided when to visit Tokyo Disney Resort, the next step is figuring out how to get there. Luckily, the Resort is well-connected to Tokyo's extensive transportation system, making getting to the airport or any part of the city easy. Here's how to make your journey stress-free:

From Tokyo Airports to the Resort

Two leading international airports serve Tokyo: **Narita International Airport (NRT)** and **Haneda Airport (HND)**. Both airports are relatively easy to reach from Tokyo Disney Resort.

1. **From Narita International Airport (NRT)**
    - **Airport Limousine Bus**: The most direct option for getting to the Resort is the **bus**, which runs directly from Narita

Airport to the Disney Resort. The bus ride takes about **60–90 minutes**, depending on traffic.

- **Train (JR Narita Express)**: You can also take the **Narita Express (N'EX)** to Tokyo Station and then transfer to the **JR Keiyo Line** to Maihama Station (the nearest station to Tokyo Disney Resort). The entire trip takes about **90 minutes**.

- **Taxi**: A taxi ride from Narita Airport to Tokyo Disney Resort takes about **60 minutes** and costs around **¥20,000–¥25,000**.

2. **From Haneda Airport (HND)**

    - **Airport Limousine Bus**: Limousine Bus services from Haneda Airport to Tokyo Disney Resort take about **40–50 minutes**.

    - **Train (Keikyu Line)**: Take the **Keikyu Line** to Shinagawa Station, then transfer to the **JR Keiyo Line** to Maihama Station. This takes about **40–45 minutes**.

    - **Taxi**: A taxi from Haneda Airport to Tokyo Disney Resort will take **30–40 minutes** and cost around **¥8,000–¥10,000**.

Transportation Around Tokyo Disney Resort

Once you've arrived at Tokyo Disney Resort, getting around is simple. Many convenient options help you navigate the parks and nearby areas.

1. **Disney Resort Line**
   - The **Disney Resort Line** is a monorail that loops around the Tokyo Disney Resort area, connecting the parks, hotels, and shopping districts. It's a fun and efficient way to get around, and it's included in the **Disney Resort Line Pass**, which gives unlimited daily rides.

2. **Walking**
   - **Tokyo Disneyland** and **Tokyo DisneySea** are within walking distance of each other. You can easily walk from one park to another or to various hotels and dining areas within the Resort.

3. **Buses and Shuttles**
   - For guests staying at Tokyo Disney Resort hotels, complimentary shuttle buses are available to transport them between the hotels and the parks.

4. **Taxis**
   - Taxis are readily available around Tokyo Disney Resort. If you're staying outside

the Resort and must reach the parks, a taxi can be a convenient option, though it is typically more expensive than public transport.

5. **Rental Bicycles**
   - Tokyo Disney Resort also offers **bicycle rentals** at some hotels, making it easy to explore the resort grounds at your own pace. Biking is a great way to get around the nearby shopping areas and resorts while enjoying the scenery.

Accommodation Options Near Tokyo Disney Resort

You have various options when finding the right place to stay near Tokyo Disney Resort. Whether you're looking for luxury, convenience, or budget-friendly choices, there's something for every type of traveler. In this section, I'll break down your options to help you make the best choice for your stay.

Disney Hotels and Resorts

Staying at a **Disney hotel** adds more magic to your Tokyo Disney Resort experience. Disney hotels are conveniently located close to the parks and offer exclusive benefits such as early park entry, character dining, and themed rooms. Here's a look at the central Disney hotels:

1. **Tokyo Disneyland Hotel**
   - **Theme**: Classic Disney, with Victorian-style decor inspired by Disneyland's iconic hotel.
   - **Location**: Just a short walk from **Tokyo Disneyland**.
   - **Amenities**: Character-themed rooms, fine dining, and luxury spa services.
   - **Special Perks**: Early Park entry and priority reservations at the park's most popular restaurants.
   - **Price Range**: ¥30,000–¥70,000 per night, depending on room type and season.

2. **Disney's Ambassador Hotel**
   - **Theme**: Art Deco, with a retro Disney flair.
   - **Location**: Located between **Tokyo Disneyland** and **Tokyo DisneySea**.
   - **Amenities**: Pool, fitness center, and character dining experiences.
   - **Special Perks**: Early park entry, themed rooms, and exclusive Disney character meet-and-greets.
   - **Price Range**: ¥25,000–¥50,000 per night.

3. **Disney's Hotel MiraCosta**
   - **Theme**: Mediterranean, directly inside **Tokyo DisneySea**.
   - **Location**: The only Disney hotel built inside a Disney Park (Tokyo DisneySea), making it the most exclusive hotel.
   - **Amenities**: Stunning views of DisneySea, luxurious rooms, top-tier dining options, and exclusive park access.
   - **Special Perks**: Early Park entry, VIP tours, and prime viewing spots for parades and fireworks.
   - **Price Range**: ¥40,000–¥80,000 per night.

4. **Tokyo Disney Celebration Hotel**
   - **Theme**: Colorful Disney celebrations with a more affordable price tag.
   - **Location**: A bit farther from the parks (about a 15-minute shuttle ride).
   - **Amenities**: Fun, family-friendly rooms with Disney themes, shuttle service to the parks, and a more budget-conscious option.
   - **Special Perks**: Early Park entry and fun character experiences.
   - **Price Range**: ¥15,000–¥25,000 per night.

Nearby Hotels for Every Budget

If you prefer to stay outside the Disney properties or are looking for more budget-friendly options, several hotels in the surrounding area are just a short distance from the parks. Here are some top choices across different price points:

1. **Luxury Options**
    - **Sheraton Grande Tokyo Bay Hotel**
        - **Location**: Just outside the Resort, with easy access to both parks.
        - **Amenities**: Luxurious rooms, various dining options, a large swimming pool, and a fitness center.
        - **Price Range**: ¥25,000–¥50,000 per night.
    - **Tokyo Bay Maihama Hotel**
        - **Location**: Located near Maihama Station, with easy access to Tokyo Disneyland and Tokyo DisneySea.
        - **Amenities**: Comfortable rooms, great for families, and various dining options.
        - **Price Range**: ¥20,000–¥40,000 per night.

2. **Mid-Range Options**
   - **Hotel Okura Tokyo Bay**
     - **Location**: Near the Resort with quick access via shuttle service.
     - **Amenities**: Spacious rooms, family-friendly options, and beautiful bay views.
     - **Price Range**: ¥15,000–¥30,000 per night.
   - **Hotel Dream Gate Maihama**
     - **Location**: Conveniently located right near Maihama Station, with quick access to the parks.
     - **Amenities**: Comfortable rooms with a slightly more affordable price tag.
     - **Price Range**: ¥12,000–¥20,000 per night.
3. **Budget-Friendly Options**
   - **APA Hotel & Resort Tokyo Bay Makuhari**
     - **Location**: A little further from the Resort but within a reasonable distance.
     - **Amenities**: Compact, functional rooms with everything you need for a comfortable stay.

- **Price Range**: ¥7,000–¥12,000 per night.
- Toyoko Inn Tokyo Disney Resort
    - **Location**: About a 15-minute shuttle ride from the Resort.
    - **Amenities**: Clean and simple rooms with basic amenities, ideal for those looking to spend more time at the parks than in the hotel room.
    - **Price Range**: ¥6,000–¥10,000 per night.

Best Family-Friendly, Couple-Friendly, and Solo Traveler Hotels

1. **Best for Families**:
    - **Tokyo Disneyland Hotel**: With its spacious rooms and luxurious amenities, families can enjoy Disney-themed rooms and easy access to the parks.
    - **Tokyo Bay Maihama Hotel**: Offers larger rooms with the convenience of being close to the parks, making it ideal for families who want comfort and value.
2. **Best for Couples**:
    - **Disney's Hotel MiraCosta**: For a romantic getaway with breathtaking

views of DisneySea, luxurious rooms, and intimate fine dining options.

- **Sheraton Grande Tokyo Bay Hotel**: With beautiful ocean views and a peaceful, tranquil atmosphere, this hotel offers an elegant, romantic stay.

3. **Best for Solo Travelers**:

    - **APA Hotel & Resort Tokyo Bay Makuhari** is for solo travelers who want an affordable, efficient place to stay close to the Resort's action.

    - **Hotel Okura Tokyo Bay**: Comfortable, accessible, and close enough to easily explore the park. The rooms are simple, clean, and perfect for a solo retreat.

Budgeting Your Trip

Now that you've decided where to stay let's discuss how to budget for your Tokyo Disney Resort vacation. A trip to this magical destination doesn't have to break the bank, but knowing what to expect regarding costs is essential. Here, I'll break down the main expenses you'll encounter during your trip.

Estimated Costs (Tickets, Food, Souvenirs, etc.)

1. **Ticket Prices**
   - **Single-Day Ticket (Tokyo Disneyland or Tokyo DisneySea):**
     - Adult (12 years and older): **¥7,900–¥8,200**
     - Child (4–11 years old): **¥5,300–¥5,500**
     - Senior (65 years and older): **¥6,900–¥7,200**
   - **Multi-Day Ticket** (usually for 2 or more days):
     - 2-Day Passport:
       - Adult: **¥13,400–¥13,800**
       - Child: **¥9,300–¥9,600**
     - 3-Day Passport:
       - Adult: **¥18,400–¥19,000**
       - Child: **¥12,500–¥13,000**

2. **Food Costs**
    - **Quick Service Meals**:
        - Expect to pay around **¥1,000–¥1,500** for a quick service meal (burgers, pizza, etc.).
    - **Table Service Meals**:
        - The cost of table service restaurants ranges between **¥2,000 and ¥4,000** per person, depending on the type of restaurant (character dining experiences can cost more).
    - **Snacks and Drinks**:
        - A snack such as churros or popcorn will cost around **¥400–¥700**.
        - Beverages (coffee, soda) will cost between **¥300–¥500**.
3. **Souvenirs**
    - **Small Souvenirs (keychains, pins, etc.)**: **¥500–¥2,000**.
    - **Apparel (t-shirts, hoodies, etc.)**: **¥2,000–¥5,000**.
    - **Exclusive Collectibles**: Expect to pay **¥3,000–¥10,000** for special event merchandise for limited-edition items.

Money-Saving Tips for a Disney Vacation

1. **Buy Tickets in Advance**: Purchasing your tickets ahead of time online or through special packages can save you money and time. Many third-party websites offer discounts or packages that include hotels and tickets at a lower price than purchasing separately.

2. **Bring Your Own Snacks**: While there are plenty of delicious snacks and meals to enjoy at the park, bringing your own snacks can help you save money. Pack granola bars, fruit, and bottled water to stay energized without overspending.

3. **Share Meals**: Many of the park's restaurants have large portion sizes. If traveling with family or friends, consider sharing meals to save money. You'll still enjoy the food but at a fraction of the cost.

4. **Use the Disney Resort Line**: The **Disney Resort Line** is a cost-effective way to travel around the resort area. The one-day pass is much more affordable than taxis and gives you unlimited access to the monorail.

5. **Take Advantage of Free Entertainment**: Tokyo Disney Resort offers incredible parades and shows, many of which are included with park admission. You can enjoy fantastic entertainment without spending a penny extra.

6. **Look for Discount Stores**: In the nearby Urayasu area, discount stores sell Disney-themed merchandise at a much lower price than in the parks. Be sure to explore these options before you head into the parks to purchase souvenirs.

7. **Plan Your Meals**: Dining reservations for character meals and popular restaurants can fill up quickly, but if you plan ahead, you'll have better chances at securing a reservation for the most affordable and fun options.

Special Offers and Deals

1. **Seasonal Promotions**
   - Tokyo Disney Resort often runs special promotions during low seasons (typically January to early March or the middle of September). These promotions can include discounted tickets or hotel packages.

2. **Multi-Park Passes**
   - If you plan on visiting Tokyo Disneyland and Tokyo DisneySea, consider purchasing a multi-day ticket or a **2-Park Pass**, which offers savings when buying tickets for multiple days or parks.

3. **Hotel Packages**
   - Many hotels near the resort offer **discounted hotel and ticket packages**. Booking these packages in advance often

includes perks like breakfast or early park entry, so check for those deals.

4. **Discounts for Japan Residents**
    - If you're a resident of Japan, be sure to look for **Japanese Resident Discounted Tickets** for Tokyo Disney Resort, which can save you a significant amount on ticket prices.

Attractions

Tokyo Disney Resort is home to two of the most magical parks in the world: **Tokyo Disneyland** and **Tokyo DisneySea**. With something for everyone—whether you're visiting as a family, couple, or solo adventurer—these parks offer a wide range of thrilling rides, immersive shows, and unforgettable experiences. Let me guide you through the top attractions you won't want to miss, along with the special events and seasonal features that will make your visit in 2025 genuinely unforgettable.

Tokyo Disneyland

Must-See Attractions

Tokyo Disneyland blends classic Disney charm with thrilling rides and immersive experiences. Here's a rundown of the must-see attractions that will make your visit magical:

1. **Pirates of the Caribbean**
   - **Why You Can't-Miss It**: Step into a world of adventure with Captain Jack Sparrow and his swashbuckling crew. This indoor boat ride takes you through a vividly detailed pirate world with pirates singing, plotting, and engaging in the ultimate pirate escapades.
   - **Must-See Detail**: The atmosphere is perfect for kids and adults, with intricate sets

and surprises around every corner. It's one of Disney's most iconic rides and the epitome of Disney's storytelling magic.

2. **Splash Mountain**

    - **Why You Can't MissCan't Miss It** is a fun, exciting log-flume ride that combines thrills with whimsical Disney storytelling. The ride takes you through the Br'er Rabbit's adventure and ends with an exhilarating plunge into the splash zone.

    - **Must-See Detail**: The 5-story drop at the end is the highlight, so prepare to get wet! It's an exciting ride perfect for families and couples looking for a mix of adventure and laughter.

3. **Big Thunder Mountain**

    - **Why You Can't-Miss It**: This classic Disney roller coaster is set in the Wild West and features a runaway mine train that twists and turns through rocky terrain. It's a must for adrenaline seekers.

    - **Must-See Detail**: Known for its sharp turns and sudden drops, it's a fantastic thrill ride with excellent theming that makes you feel deep in the mountains.

4. **Space Mountain**
    - **Why You Can't Miss It**: A high-speed, indoor roller coaster that simulates a journey through outer space. Space Mountain combines darkness, dazzling lights, and gravity-defying loops for a heart-pounding adventure out of this world.
    - **Must-See Detail**: The dark twists and the sense of flying through the galaxy make this ride a true Disney classic, loved by thrill-seekers and space enthusiasts.

5. **It's a Small World**
    - **Why You Can't Miss It**: This iconic boat ride is a tribute to global unity and a soothing, colorful escape. With its catchy tune and adorable dolls from all over the world, it is the ride to take a break from the thrills and immerse yourself in the classic Disney spirit.
    - **Must-See Detail**: The whimsical characters and vibrant colors make this attraction magical for children and adults who appreciate its timeless charm.

Top Rides for Families, Couples, and Solo Travelers

Tokyo Disneyland is a haven for families, couples, and solo travelers, offering a variety of attractions suited to all preferences:

1. **For Families**:

    - **Pooh's Hunny Hunt**: This cutting-edge, trackless ride takes families through the Hundred Acre Wood with Winnie the Pooh. It's fun, gentle, and full of heartwarming moments.

    - **The Enchanted Tiki Room**: A delightful show featuring animatronic birds, flowers, and tikis. This is a great place to relax and enjoy the whimsical Disney magic with young kids.

2. **For Couples**:

    - **The Haunted Mansion**: Perfect for couples who enjoy spooky, fun experiences. The Haunted Mansion is filled with hauntingly beautiful décor and a touch of eerie magic, making it a perfect evening date for a bit of thrill and fun.

    - **Cinderella's Castle Walkthrough**: For a romantic, quieter experience, wander through the majestic **Cinderella Castle** and explore its charming interiors, which are full of fairy-tale wonders and magical ambiance.

3. **For Solo Travelers**:

    - **Star Tours – The Adventures Continue**: This thrilling flight simulator based on the Star Wars universe offers multiple storylines and is perfect for solo adventurers looking to immerse themselves in the epic battles of the galaxy.

- **Monsters, Inc. Ride & Go Seek** is a fun interactive attraction where you hunt for hidden monsters using a flashlight. It's great for solo travelers who want a more engaging, participatory experience.

Iconic Shows and Parades

1. **Dreaming Up! Parade**

    - **Why You Can't-Miss It**: This daytime parade features Disney characters, colorful floats, and energetic music. It's the perfect way to experience Disney magic in the middle of the day.

    - **Must-See Detail**: The parade features classic Disney characters and new favorites, so it's an excellent option for Disney fans of all ages.

2. **Nighttime Spectacular: "Believe! Sea of Dreams"**

    - **Why You Can't-Miss It**: This nighttime fireworks and water projection show brings Disney's magic to life with spectacular visuals, heartwarming moments, and fireworks.

    - **Must-See Detail**: The show incorporates beloved Disney films and characters, creating a powerful emotional experience while lighting up the night sky above the castle.

Seasonal and Special Attractions for 2025

1. **Halloween (September – October)**
   - Special Halloween parades, decorations, and exclusive character meet-and-greets. You'll encounter Disney villains, spooky music, and special treats, making the whole park feel like a magical haunted mansion.

2. **Christmas (November – December)**
   - The Christmas celebration at Tokyo Disneyland is an absolute must-see. Expect festive decorations, special Christmas parades, and exclusive holiday merchandise. The **"Christmas Fantasy" Parade** features Disney characters in their holiday attire and a fabulous festive atmosphere.

Tokyo DisneySea

Tokyo DisneySea offers an entirely different experience with a unique nautical theme that can't be found in any other Disney Park worldwide. The park is divided into different themed lands, each offering its own set of attractions, shows, and dining options.

Overview of DisneySea's Themed Lands

1. **Mediterranean Harbor**
   - This beautiful area, which resembles an Italian seaside village, is the entry point to the park. The stunning architecture, gondola rides, and waterfront restaurants make it a perfect place for couples and families.

2. **American Waterfront**
   - Inspired by the American Northeast, this area includes **Tower of Terror** and **Toy Story Mania**. It's full of Americana, with stunning details and delicious dining spots.

3. **Port Discovery**
   - The future is alive at Port Discovery, home to high-tech attractions like **StormRider** and the futuristic **Aquatopia** ride. This is an excellent place for thrill-seekers and families looking for interactive experiences.

4. **Lost River Delta**
   - Explore a jungle ruin filled with ancient secrets. **Indiana Jones Adventure: Temple of the Crystal Skull** is one of the park's most thrilling rides, offering an exciting escape into the world of adventure.

5. **Mysterious Island**
   - This land is built around **Mount Prometheus** and inspired by Jules Verne's works. The **Journey to the Center of the Earth** and **20,000 Leagues Under the Sea** rides offer thrilling adventures through this mysterious and dramatic landscape.

6. **Arabian Coast**
   - Transport yourself to the Arabian world with exotic architecture, a magic carpet ride, and delicious Middle Eastern-inspired food. **Sinbad's Storybook Voyage** is a charming boat ride through the tales of Sinbad.

7. **Fantasy Springs (2025 debut)**
   - In 2025, **Fantasy Springs** will bring to life the magical worlds of Disney's animated classics such as **Frozen**, **Tangled**, and **Peter Pan**. Expect breathtaking new attractions and experiences that enchant families and Disney fans.

Best Rides and Attractions at DisneySea

1. **Journey to the Center of the Earth**
   - **Why You Can't Miss It**: This ride is a DisneySea exclusive. It takes you on a thrilling journey through the Earth's core,

with impressive visuals and exhilarating drops.

- **Must-See Detail**: The experience is unique, blending suspense, beautiful theming, and unforgettable thrilling moments.

2. **Tower of Terror**

    - **Why You Can't Miss It**: DisneySea's version of the Tower of Terror offers a terrifyingly fun freefall experience and a rich storyline that immerses you in its haunted history.

    - **Must-See Detail**: The hotel's eerie theme, detailed storytelling, and thrilling drop make it one of the park's top attractions.

3. **Indiana Jones Adventure: Temple of the Crystal Skull**

    - **Why You Can't Miss It**: This ride is necessary for thrill-seekers and adventure lovers. It offers a wild, action-packed experience with high-speed twists and turns.

    - **Must-See Detail**: The ride's theming is incredible, combining motion, storytelling, and incredible special effects.

-

Exclusive Shows and Events at DisneySea

1. **Fantasmic!**
   - **Why You Can't Miss It**: This incredible nighttime show at Mediterranean Harbor combines fireworks, water projections, and Disney characters in a spectacular performance that blends fantasy and reality.
   - **Must-See Detail**: The show's dramatic visuals and high-energy performances make it an essential part of your DisneySea visit.

2. **Big Band Beat**
   - **Why You Can't Miss It**: A lively, jazz-filled show that features Mickey and the gang swinging to big band tunes. It's a fantastic performance for couples and solo travelers who appreciate a touch of old-school Disney magic.

Attractions by Age Group

Best Attractions for Young Kids

Tokyo Disney Resort is designed to delight children with gentle rides, colorful characters, and interactive experiences perfect for younger visitors. If you're visiting with little ones, these attractions are the best options to keep them entertained and enchanted throughout the day.

1. **Pooh's Hunny Hunt (Tokyo Disneyland)**
   - **Why It's Perfect for Kids**: This trackless ride takes children on a delightful adventure through the Hundred Acre Wood, where they'll meet Winnie the Pooh and friends. The whimsical, colorful scenes and gentle pace make it a favorite for young children.
   - **Must-See Detail**: Kids will love the interactive nature of the ride as they explore Pooh's world, encountering honey pots and playful characters along the way. It's a magical experience that brings the beloved characters to life!

2. **The Many Adventures of Winnie the Pooh (Tokyo Disneyland)**
   - **Why It's Perfect for Kids**: For a more classic ride, this one lets children board "honey pots" as they journey through the scenes from the Winnie the Pooh storybook. The smooth, flowing pace and vibrant visuals are ideal for younger visitors.
   - **Must-See Detail**: The bright colors, soft music, and familiar faces create a soothing experience that kids of all ages will enjoy.

3. **It's a Small World (Tokyo Disneyland)**
   - **Why It's Perfect for Kids**: This iconic boat ride offers a gentle, immersive journey

through different countries, filled with cute dolls singing the famous "It's a Small World" song. It's a celebration of cultures that younger children will find fascinating.

- **Must-See Detail**: The large, colorful animatronic dolls, the catchy tune, and the lighthearted mood make it a family favorite that appeals to young children. Plus, it's a great way to relax while exploring the park.

4. **Dumbo the Flying Elephant (Tokyo Disneyland)**

   - **Why It's Perfect for Kids**: A classic Disney ride where kids can control their own flying Dumbo! This gentle flying ride is a must-do for young children and an excellent opportunity to view the park from a bird's-eye view.

   - **Must-See Detail**: The bright colors and whimsical design make it visually exciting for young ones, while the simplicity and control make it a fun, gentle ride for even the tiniest guests.

5. **Monsters, Inc. Ride & Go Seek (Tokyo Disneyland)**

   - **Why It's Perfect for Kids**: This interactive dark ride uses flashlights to find and identify different monsters, making it an engaging and fun experience for young ones. It's also an excellent way to get kids involved and excited about the ride.

- **Must-See Detail**: The playful interaction, bright colors, and lovable characters from the *Monsters, Inc.* movie ensure that kids stay entertained and engaged.

Teen-Friendly and Thrill-Seeking Rides

For older kids and teens looking for more adventure and excitement, Tokyo Disney Resort has an array of thrilling rides that will get their adrenaline pumping. These rides combine high-speed thrills with immersive theming, offering an experience that's as exciting as it is memorable.

1. **Big Thunder Mountain (Tokyo Disneyland)**
   - **Why It's Perfect for Teens**: This thrilling roller coaster takes you through the wild, untamed wilderness on a runaway mine train. It's fast and bumpy, perfect for those seeking thrills with a bit of Wild West adventure.
   - **Must-See Detail**: The sharp turns, sudden drops, and exciting ride pace make it an excellent option for teens. The theming of the old western mining town adds extra fun to the experience.

2. **Space Mountain (Tokyo Disneyland)**
   - **Why It's Perfect for Teens**: Space Mountain is a must-ride for teens who love

thrills! This high-speed roller coaster sends guests on a thrilling adventure through outer space in near darkness.

- **Must-See Detail**: The feeling of speeding through space, with sudden drops and tight turns, will definitely get your heart racing. It's one of the park's most iconic rides and a fan favorite.

3. **Indiana Jones Adventure: Temple of the Crystal Skull (Tokyo DisneySea)**

    - **Why It's Perfect for Teens**: This adventure, based on the *Indiana Jones* films, is a wild ride through dangerous ruins filled with traps and surprises. It's fast, thrilling, and perfect for teens seeking action-packed fun.

    - **Must-See Detail**: With all the perilous encounters and sudden drops, the ride's theming creates an exciting experience that will surely thrill even the most adventurous teens.

4. **Tower of Terror (Tokyo DisneySea)**

    - **Why It's Perfect for Teens**: **Tower of Terror** is the perfect ride if your teen enjoys a good scare. This haunted hotel elevator ride has spooky thrills, sudden drops, and chilling moments.

    - **Must-See Detail**: The terrifying theming, sudden freefall drops, and eerie suspense will keep teens on the edge of their seats.

5. **Raging Spirits (Tokyo DisneySea)**
   - **Why It's Perfect for Teens**: This roller coaster features sharp turns, unexpected twists, and a thrilling loop! Based in the jungles of a mysterious archaeological site, it offers a perfect blend of ancient adventure and high-speed thrills.
   - **Must-See Detail**: The loop and high-speed portions of this ride will keep adrenaline junkies excited, while the jungle-themed surroundings make it feel like an actual treasure hunt.

Fun for Adults and Seniors

While Tokyo Disney Resort is geared toward families and young children, adults and seniors also have plenty of attractions to enjoy. Whether you're looking for an immersive experience, a chance to relax, or a more scenic, laid-back adventure, here are the top rides and experiences for adults and seniors.

1. **The Enchanted Tiki Room (Tokyo Disneyland)**
   - **Why It's Perfect for Adults and Seniors**: This charming, relaxing show features animatronic birds and lush tropical landscapes. It's a delightful break from the fast-paced attractions and an excellent choice for those looking to relax and enjoy a leisurely experience.

- **Must-See Detail**: The vibrant colors, sweet melodies, and quirky bird characters make this show nostalgic and fun for all ages.

2. **Journey to the Center of the Earth (Tokyo DisneySea)**

    - **Why It's Perfect for Adults and Seniors**: **Journey to the Center of the Earth** is a must-see for adults who love a thrilling yet immersive adventure. It's a visually stunning ride that takes you deep into the Earth's core, with amazing effects and a thrilling surprise at the end.

    - **Must-See Detail**: The blend of breathtaking visuals and mild thrills makes it perfect for adults looking for a balanced adventure.

3. **Sinbad's Storybook Voyage (Tokyo DisneySea)**

    - **Why It's Perfect for Adults and Seniors**: This gentle boat ride takes you through the legendary stories of Sinbad. Its colorful, serene atmosphere and beautiful storytelling make it a relaxing ride for those who prefer a slower pace.

    - **Must-See Detail**: The rich, exotic settings, calming pace, and vibrant characters make this a perfect choice for seniors and adults seeking relaxation at DisneySea.

4. **The Magic Lamp Theater (Tokyo DisneySea)**

   - **Why It's Perfect for Adults and Seniors**: This immersive, air-conditioned show combines 3D effects with live-action storytelling based on *Aladdin*. It's an excellent way for adults and seniors to unwind while still experiencing the magic of Disney.

   - **Must-See Detail**: The combination of cutting-edge technology, humor, and Disney magic makes it an enjoyable show for adults who appreciate engaging and interactive entertainment.

5. **Cinderella's Castle Walkthrough (Tokyo Disneyland)**

   - **Why It's Perfect for Adults and Seniors**: Explore the story of Cinderella in a tranquil walk through the castle, admiring the beautiful stained-glass windows and intricate details that bring the classic tale to life.

   - **Must-See Detail**: It's a peaceful, picturesque experience perfect for those who want to enjoy the park's charm without the hustle and bustle of rides.

Top Attractions for Families, Couples, and Solo Travelers

1. **For Families**:
   - **Pirates of the Caribbean (Tokyo Disneyland)**: This thrilling yet family-friendly boat ride is perfect for families with kids of all ages. It's exciting but not too intense for younger children and offers enough adventure to entertain older kids and adults.
   - **Monsters, Inc. Ride & Go Seek (Tokyo Disneyland)**: This interactive experience is ideal for families. With its playful monster characters and scavenger hunt-style fun, it's an experience everyone can enjoy together.

2. **For Couples**:
   - **Big Thunder Mountain (Tokyo Disneyland)**: Couples can bond over the excitement and thrill of this wild roller coaster, with its unexpected twists and turns through a scenic western town.
   - **Journey to the Center of the Earth (Tokyo DisneySea)**: With its stunning visuals and thrilling adventure, this ride is perfect for couples who enjoy immersive storytelling and scenic experiences.

3. **For Solo Travelers**:
    - **Star Tours – The Adventures Continue (Tokyo Disneyland)**: Solo travelers can enjoy this thrilling ride, which takes them through various Star Wars scenes and allows for a solo, engaging experience.
    - **Sinbad's Storybook Voyage (Tokyo DisneySea)** is a calm and relaxing boat ride ideal for solo travelers looking to unwind. It offers an immersive journey through beautiful settings without the rush of big crowds.

Dining

Tokyo Disney Resort isn't just a magical destination for rides and attractions—it's a culinary adventure waiting to be discovered! Whether looking for a quick snack to fuel your day, a themed experience with your favorite Disney characters, or a romantic dinner in a luxurious setting, the Resort offers various dining options to suit every taste and preference. Let me take you on a delicious journey through some of the best dining experiences at the Resort, with options for families, couples, and solo travelers.

Best Restaurants for Families, Couples, and Solo Travelers

Tokyo Disney Resort offers a wide range of dining options that cater to everyone, whether you're here with the whole family, as a couple, or exploring solo. Here are some must-try options for every type of traveler:

Character Dining Experiences

Character dining is one of the most magical and memorable experiences for families visiting Tokyo Disney Resort. These meals offer the chance to dine with beloved Disney characters, creating a unique, interactive dining experience.

1. **Chef Mickey (Disney's Disney Ambassador Hotel)**
   - **Why It's Perfect for Families**: Chef Mickey is one of the Resort's most iconic character dining experiences. Kids and adults alike can interact with Mickey Mouse and friends while enjoying a buffet-style meal.
   - **Cuisine**: International buffet featuring everything from fresh seafood to Asian and Western dishes.
   - **What Makes It Special**: Besides meeting Mickey and his friends, the vibrant atmosphere and the opportunity to snap photos with characters make it a family favorite.
   - **Must-Try**: The sushi and fresh seafood are standout items, alongside the hearty, comforting dishes like roasted meats and themed desserts.

2. **Plaza Restaurant (Tokyo Disneyland)**
   - **Why It's Perfect for Families**: Located in the park's heart, Plaza Restaurant offers a delightful character dining experience with popular Disney characters such as Goofy, Chip, and Dale while enjoying a delicious buffet.
   - **Cuisine**: Western-style dishes like roast chicken, pasta, salads, and desserts.

- **What Makes It Special**: The lively atmosphere and interactions with characters are great for families with younger children who love the Disney characters.
- **Must-Try**: The hearty roast dishes and the character-shaped desserts are always a hit with kids.

3. **Aloha Isle (Tokyo Disneyland)**
   - **Why It's Perfect for Families**: This tropical-themed quick-service spot offers a more relaxed setting for meeting Disney friends, particularly for families who want to grab a quick bite without sacrificing character experiences.
   - **Cuisine**: Refreshing tropical snacks and light bites such as Dole Whip (a refreshing frozen dessert).
   - **What Makes It Special**: Aloha Isle's laid-back atmosphere allows families to unwind and indulge in delicious tropical desserts while soaking up the atmosphere.
   - **Must-Try**: The famous Dole Whip is a must-try for any Disney fan, especially in the warm summer.

Themed Restaurants

Themed restaurants at Tokyo Disney Resort immerse you in various Disney worlds, offering delicious food and a unique atmosphere. These dining spots let you enter a Disney movie or fantasy world, where the décor and cuisine reflect the theme.

1. **Magellan's (Tokyo DisneySea)**
   - **Why It's Perfect for Couples**: Magellan's is an elegant, fine-dining restaurant in DisneySea's beautiful Fortress Explorations. The intimate setting is perfect for couples seeking a special night out.
   - **Cuisine**: Mediterranean and international-inspired dishes with fresh, high-quality ingredients.
   - **What Makes It Special**: The restaurant's luxurious atmosphere is designed to resemble a 16th-century explorer's club, complete with antique maps and artifacts, making it perfect for a romantic dinner.
   - **Must-Try**: The delectable steaks and the wine list are out here, providing a truly sophisticated dining experience.

2. **S.S. Columbia Dining Room (Tokyo DisneySea)**
   - **Why It's Perfect for Couples and Solo Travelers**: The S.S. Columbia offers a fine dining experience on board a luxurious replica ocean liner. With sweeping views of the harbor, this is ideal for couples and solo travelers who want to indulge in an elegant setting.

- **Cuisine**: American cuisine with premium meat, seafood, and seasonal vegetable cuts.
- **What Makes It Special**: The stunning, upscale atmosphere of the dining room aboard the S.S. Columbia, combined with breathtaking views of the American Waterfront, creates a truly memorable experience.
- **Must-Try**: The filet mignon and lobster tail are excellent choices for those looking for an indulgent meal.

3. **Ristorante di Canaletto (Tokyo DisneySea)**
    - **Why It's Perfect for Couples**: For a taste of Italy in the heart of DisneySea, Ristorante di Canaletto offers a charming and romantic Italian dining experience along the Venetian canals.
    - **Cuisine**: Traditional Italian fare with pizza, pasta, and rich, flavorful sauces.
    - **What Makes It Special**: The romantic atmosphere, waterfront views, and beautiful setting make this the ideal spot for a date night or a leisurely meal with family.
    - **Must-Try**: The handmade pasta dishes and the classic Italian tiramisu are perfect for anyone craving authentic Italian flavors.

Quick Service vs. Fine Dining

When dining at Tokyo Disney Resort, there's something for every budget and schedule. Whether you're looking for a quick bite between attractions or a leisurely fine-dining experience, the Resort has plenty of options to cater to your needs.

Quick Service Dining

1. **Grandma Sara's Kitchen (Tokyo Disneyland)**
    - **Why It's Great for Families**: This rustic, homestyle kitchen serves comforting Japanese and Western fusion meals, making it perfect for families who want something filling and quick without sacrificing taste.
    - **Cuisine**: A combination of Japanese rice dishes, fried chicken, and Western-style set meals.
    - **Must-Try**: The fried chicken and Japanese curry rice are delicious, and the portions are generous.

2. **Casbah Food Court (Tokyo DisneySea)**
    - **Why It's Great for Solo Travelers and Couples**: If you're on the go or looking for a convenient bite, Casbah Food Court offers a variety of quick-service Mediterranean-inspired options in a beautiful setting.

- **Cuisine**: Mediterranean wraps, grilled meats, and light, healthy options like salads and rice bowls.
- **Must-Try**: The lamb kebabs and couscous are flavorful, and the salads are fresh and satisfying.

Fine Dining

1. **Hokusai (Tokyo Disneyland Hotel)**
   - **Why It's Great for Adults and Couples**: Located in the Tokyo Disneyland Hotel, Hokusai offers an upscale Japanese dining experience in an elegant, quiet atmosphere.
   - **Cuisine**: Traditional Japanese dishes emphasizing sushi, sashimi, and fresh seafood.
   - **Must-Try**: The omakase (chef's choice) sushi platter is a must for sushi lovers. It offers a range of delicate, expertly prepared pieces.

2. **The Blue Lagoon Restaurant (Tokyo DisneySea)**
   - **Why It's Great for Families and Couples**: This uniquely themed restaurant offers diners the chance to enjoy a meal inside a hidden pirate's lair. The calm, intimate ambiance is perfect for families or romantic evenings.

- **Cuisine**: French and Mediterranean-inspired dishes featuring grilled meats and seafood.
- **Must-Try**: The seafood platters and French-inspired appetizers are full of fresh flavors, and the desserts are decadent.

Dining Plans and Reservations

Dining at Tokyo Disney Resort can be a wonderful part of your experience, but securing a spot at your favorite restaurant is essential to the Resort's popularity. Here's everything you need to know about making dining reservations and understanding the dining plans available at the Resort.

How to Make Dining Reservations

1. **Online Reservations**
   - Tokyo Disney Resort offers a **reservation system** through its official website and mobile app. For popular restaurants, making a reservation in advance is highly recommended, especially during peak seasons (such as weekends, holidays, and special events).
   - **How to Book**: To check availability, go to the official Tokyo Disney Resort website or use the Tokyo Disney Resort app. Then, select the restaurant, date, and time and proceed with booking.

2. **Booking Through the Hotel**
   - If you're staying at one of the Disney Resort Hotels, the hotel staff can assist you with making dining reservations. This is especially helpful if you're staying in one of the Disney hotels, as they often get priority bookings for specific restaurants.

3. **At the Restaurant**
   - No reservation is needed for quick-service options. Simply walk up and order your food. If availability permits, you can often make same-day reservations for sit-down restaurants, but they are generally more limited.

Disney Dining Plans (If Available)

As of 2025, Tokyo Disney Resort does not offer an official **dining plan** like some Disney resorts (such as Walt Disney World). However, there are still ways to save money and plan your meals effectively:

1. **Meal Coupons**
   - Some hotels and third-party vendors offer **meal coupons** or "set meal packages," which allow you to enjoy meals at select restaurants for a fixed price. These can be a good way to save if you're planning to dine at certain quick-service or themed restaurants.

2. **Hotel Meal Packages**
   - Certain Disney hotels may offer **meal packages** that include breakfast, lunch, or dinner as part of your stay. This is particularly convenient for those who want to plan their meals ahead of time.

3. **Special Event Dining**
   - During seasonal events (like Halloween or Christmas), **exclusive dining experiences**, such as themed dinners or buffet options, often provide a unique dining experience. Keep an eye out for these special deals during your visit.

Hidden Dining Gems

While it's easy to get caught up in the hustle and bustle of the leading restaurants and popular quick-service spots, Tokyo Disney Resort has some **hidden gems** where you can enjoy delicious meals in peaceful and often less crowded settings. Let me share some of my favorite off-the-beaten-path dining spots that offer unique atmospheres and delightful meals.

Off-the-Beaten-Path Restaurants

1. **Casbah Food Court (Tokyo DisneySea)**
   - **Location**: Nestled in the exotic Arabian Coast area of Tokyo DisneySea, this themed dining spot is often overlooked by many visitors heading toward the more popular restaurants.

- **Why It's a Hidden Gem**: It offers a quieter escape from the main attractions, with a soothing atmosphere and delicious Mediterranean-inspired food. The food court is often less crowded than other spots, especially during peak hours.

- **Cuisine**: Mediterranean fare such as couscous, grilled meats, and wraps.

- **Must-Try**: The **lamb kebabs** and **Hummus Plate** are standout dishes, perfect for anyone craving a flavorful, healthy meal.

2. **Polynesian Terrace Restaurant (Tokyo Disneyland)**

    - **Location**: Located on the second floor of the **Adventureland** area, it's tucked away from the busy pathways, making it a hidden gem.

    - **Why It's a Hidden Gem**: This Polynesian-inspired restaurant features a peaceful environment and a delightful tropical-themed menu. While it's popular among those who know about it, many guests overlook it in favor of larger-character dining experiences.

    - **Cuisine**: Tropical-inspired dishes such as sweet-and-sour chicken, grilled fish, and coconut-flavored desserts.

- **Must-Try**: The **Polynesian chicken** and **coconut rice** offer a refreshing departure from typical theme park fare.

3. **Magellan's (Tokyo DisneySea)**

    - **Location**: Tucked inside the **Mysterious Island** area of DisneySea, this fine dining restaurant is often overshadowed by its more famous counterparts but is an absolute hidden treasure.

    - **Why It's a Hidden Gem**: Magellan's luxurious, club-like interior offers a romantic atmosphere, making it perfect for a peaceful, upscale dining experience. It's a bit off the main drag, but it's worth seeking out for its exclusive, high-quality cuisine.

    - **Cuisine**: Mediterranean-inspired dishes and French cuisine, including seafood, steaks, and decadent desserts.

    - **Must-Try**: The **Beef Tenderloin** and the **chocolate soufflé** are indulgent and exquisite, making it one of the finest dining experiences at the Resort.

4. **Ristorante di Canaletto (Tokyo DisneySea)**

    - **Location**: Situated in the **Venetian-themed** area of DisneySea, Canaletto is often overshadowed by more famous themed restaurants in the area.

- **Why It's a Hidden Gem**: Despite being in a popular area, it's a calm and serene spot, perfect for those looking to take a break from the crowds. The authentic Italian cuisine and picturesque canals create a charming ambiance.
- **Cuisine**: Traditional Italian dishes such as pasta, pizza, and seasonal specials.
- **Must-Try**: The **Lasagna al Forno** and **Tiramisu** are comforting and perfectly executed, offering an authentic taste of Italy in the heart of DisneySea.

5. **Hokusai (Tokyo Disneyland Hotel)**
   - **Location**: Situated in the Tokyo Disneyland Hotel, this Japanese restaurant is a quiet gem offering an elegant atmosphere.
   - **Why It's a Hidden Gem**: Not many guests know the high-end Japanese dining available here, especially compared to the more casual dining experiences in the park. Hokusai offers a peaceful and sophisticated atmosphere away from the crowds.
   - **Cuisine**: Traditional Japanese dishes like sushi, tempura, and sashimi.
   - **Must-Try**: The **Omakase sushi** (chef's choice) offers the freshest and most flavorful fish, and the **tempura** is delicately crisped, making it a must-try for any fan of Japanese cuisine.

Unique and Secret Dining Experiences

Tokyo Disney Resort offers **exclusive secret dining experiences**, often requiring advanced booking. These hidden experiences offer an unforgettable culinary journey, perfect for those who want to indulge in something extraordinary.

1. **DisneySea's Nautilus (Tokyo DisneySea)**
   - **Location**: Hidden within the **Mysterious Island,** the Nautilus is a secret dining area designed to replicate the famous submarine from *20,000 Leagues Under the Sea*.
   - **Why It's a Secret Dining Experience**: The restaurant is tucked away inside the *Nautilus* submarine, making the experience feel like a treasure hunt. Few guests know about it, and reservations are hard to come by, but those who seek it out are rewarded with a one-of-a-kind adventure.
   - **Cuisine**: Fine dining with a nautical theme featuring fresh seafood, premium meats, and intricate Japanese-inspired dishes.
   - **Must-Try**: The **Nautilus Seafood Platter** and the **seafood bisque** are indulgent and flavorful choices that offer a taste of luxury.

2. **Mysterious Island Dinner Cruise (Tokyo DisneySea)**
    - **Location**: Boarding from **Port Discovery** in DisneySea, this unique dining experience lets you cruise around the park while enjoying a gourmet dinner on a boat.
    - **Why It's a Secret Dining Experience**: Only a few guests know about this exclusive dining option, making it a rare and intimate experience. The cruise is perfect for couples or small groups looking for a special dinner while exploring the waterways of DisneySea.
    - **Cuisine**: A multi-course meal featuring seafood, vegetables, and specialty dishes crafted by top chefs.
    - **Must-Try**: The **lobster bisque** and **pan-seared scallops** are favorites, and the dessert options are exquisite.

Must-Try Dishes at Tokyo Disney Resort

There are certain dishes that you **cannot miss** when you're at Tokyo Disney Resort. Whether indulging in a quick snack or enjoying a full-course meal, here are the must-try dishes that elevate your culinary journey.

1. **Dole Whip (Tokyo Disneyland)**
    - **Why You Can't-Miss It**: This tropical treat is a refreshing frozen dessert that has become a

worldwide beloved classic at Disney parks. The perfect combination of pineapple and creamy softness makes it a dessert and a refreshing pick-me-up in the heat.

- **Where to Find It**: Available at **Aloha Isle** in Adventureland at Tokyo Disneyland.

- **Must-Try**: The classic **pineapple Dole Whip** is a must, but for an extra twist, try the **pineapple float**, which combines the Dole Whip with refreshing pineapple juice.

2. Churros (Tokyo Disneyland & Tokyo DisneySea)

- **Why You Can't Miss It**: No trip to a Disney park is complete without a churro! Tokyo Disney Resort takes these cinnamon-sugar treats to the next level with creative flavors.

- **Where to Find It**: Churros are sold at various carts around both parks, and they come in unique seasonal flavors.

- **Must-Try**: The **maple churro** and **apple-flavored churro** are top choices, offering a twist on the classic cinnamon flavor.

3. Tony's Town Square Restaurant Pasta (Tokyo Disneyland)

- **Why You Can't Miss It**: If you're looking for a hearty, satisfying meal, Tony's Town Square's pasta dishes are a favorite. Located in the heart of Tokyo Disneyland, this Italian restaurant serves up rich pasta dishes that hit the spot after a busy day of exploring.

- **Cuisine**: Italian-inspired pasta dishes.
- **Must-Try**: The **spaghetti with meatballs** and the **risotto** are comforting and flavorful.

4. Frozen Beverages at Casbah Food Court (Tokyo DisneySea)

- **Why You Can't Miss It**: If you're visiting Tokyo DisneySea during the warmer months, a frozen beverage from the Casbah Food Court is a refreshing way to cool down. These drinks come in fun tropical flavors that perfectly complement the Mediterranean theme.
- **Where to Find It**: **Casbah Food Court** is on the Arabian Coast in Tokyo DisneySea.
- **Must-Try**: The **frozen lemon mint** drink is popular, offering a tangy and refreshing flavor.

5. Gyoza Dogs (Tokyo Disneyland)

- **Why You Can't Miss It**: One of the more unique snack offerings at Tokyo Disneyland, the Gyoza Dog is a fusion of Japanese gyoza and a hot dog, making it a must-try for adventurous eaters.
- **Where to Find It**: **Gyoza Dog Cart** near the park entrance.
- **Must-Try**: The **classic gyoza dog**, with its juicy filling wrapped in a crispy exterior, is both filling and delicious.

Shopping and Souvenirs

Shopping at Tokyo Disney Resort is like a treasure hunt that adds another layer of magic to your visit. From exclusive Disney products to personalized souvenirs, there's no shortage of unique and unforgettable items to bring home. Whether you're hunting for something special for yourself, your family, or your significant other, the Resort offers many shops and treasures waiting to be discovered. Let's dive into Disney shopping, where every corner holds a new surprise and an exclusive souvenir just for you!

Where to Shop for Disney Merchandise

Tokyo Disney Resort is brimming with exciting shops, each offering something a little different. Whether you're looking for limited-edition collectibles or everyday Disney magic, a store (or two) will cater to your every wish.

Exclusive Disney Products

If you're looking for something unique that can only be found at Tokyo Disney Resort, be sure to seek out these exclusive Disney products:

74 |TOKYO DISNEY RESORT

1. **Limited-Edition Merchandise**
   - **Where to Find It**: Various stores across both **Tokyo Disneyland** and **Tokyo DisneySea** feature limited-edition products, often tied to anniversaries, seasonal events, or newly released movies.
   - **Must-Have Items**:
     - **Limited-edition pins**: Collectible pins are always in high demand, and Tokyo Disney Resort often releases exclusive pins that are only available in limited quantities.
     - **Special edition plush toys**: Tokyo Disney Resort regularly releases exclusive plush toys featuring rare characters or themed designs tied to events and seasons. These make for great mementos or gifts for Disney collectors.
2. **Tokyo Disney Resort 40th Anniversary Merchandise (2025)**
   - **Where to Find It**: The parks, especially in the leading gift shops near Tokyo Disneyland and Tokyo DisneySea entrances.

- **Must-Have Items**:
  - **40th Anniversary-themed apparel**: Expect t-shirts, hoodies, and hats featuring exclusive artwork celebrating the Resort's 40th Anniversary.
  - **Commemorative souvenirs**: Look for special-edition mugs, photo frames, and other keepsakes that mark this milestone in Disney history. These items are perfect for commemorating your visit in 2025.

3. **Tokyo DisneySea Exclusive Products**
   - **Where to Find It**: In the shops of **Tokyo DisneySea**, especially in areas like **Mysterious Island** and **Arabian Coast**, where the park's unique, nautical themes come to life in merchandise.
   - **Must-Have Items**:
     - **Nautical-themed souvenirs**: Think ship-wheel-shaped keychains, compass-inspired jewelry, and maritime plush toys. These products reflect DisneySea's adventurous spirit and are perfect for Disney fans who love the park's one-of-a-kind theme.

Must-Buy Souvenirs and Gifts

Shopping at Tokyo Disney Resort isn't just about buying souvenirs; it's about capturing the park's essence and taking a piece of the magic home. These are some of the top souvenirs you won't want to miss.

1. **Mickey Ears and Hats**
   - **Where to Find It**: Almost every shop at Tokyo Disney Resort offers a variety of Mickey ears and themed hats, but the **World Bazaar** in Tokyo Disneyland is mainly known for its selection.
   - **Must-Have Items**:
     - **Mickey Mouse Ears**: Whether you're looking for classic Mickey ears or themed designs (think anniversary hats or seasonal special editions), these are a must-have for any Disney fan.
     - **Custom Hats**: You can find unique Disney hats representing different Disney themes, including **Pirates of the Caribbean** and **Frozen**.

2. **Exclusive Disney Pins**
   - **Where to Find It**: Pin trading is hugely popular at Tokyo Disney Resort, and you'll find an abundance of pin shops at both Disneyland and DisneySea.
   - **Must-Have Items**:
     - **Seasonal Pins**: Look for pins that commemorate the current season or event, like Halloween or Christmas,

which are only available during that time.

- **Character Pins**: If you have a favorite Disney character, chances are you'll find a pin featuring them in various designs, from classic characters like Mickey to the newest movie releases.

3. **Japanese-Inspired Disney Merchandise**

    - **Where to Find It**: Shops like **Ikspiari** (the shopping mall near the Resort) and some of the smaller boutiques at Tokyo Disneyland offer Japanese-themed Disney merchandise.

    - **Must-Have Items**:

        - **Kimonos and Yukatas**: During the summer, you can find Disney-branded yukatas (a traditional Japanese garment). These come in various Disney-themed prints and are perfect for taking home a piece of Japan with a Disney twist.

        - **Japanese Snacks and Souvenirs**: Many shops sell unique Disney-themed Japanese snacks, like **Mickey-shaped mochi** and **Disney-themed matcha-flavored treats**.

What to Buy for Families, Couples, and Solo Travelers

When finding the perfect souvenir, Tokyo Disney Resort offers something for everyone—whether shopping for the whole family, picking out a romantic gift for a partner, or treating yourself to a unique find as a solo traveler.

Personalized Gifts and Memorabilia

1. **Customized Mickey Ears and Apparel**
   - **For Families and Couples**: What could be more special than personalized Mickey ears or matching t-shirts for the whole family or couple? You can have your name, favorite Disney characters, or a special date embroidered on items.
   - **Where to Find It: The World Bazaar** at Tokyo Disneyland and special kiosks inside the parks are where you can get your customized items.

2. **Personalized Photo Frames**
   - **For Families and Solo Travelers**: Personalized photo frames are perfect for keeping a memento from your magical day at the parks. You can find frames with Disney designs and even engrave them with your name and the visit date.

- **Where to Find It**: It is available in many gift shops, including the ones near **Cinderella Castle** and **Mediterranean Harbor** in DisneySea.

3. **Engraved Jewelry**
   - **For Couples**: Check out the beautiful Disney-themed **engraved jewelry** for a romantic souvenir. These can be customized with your name, a unique Disney quote, or a memorable date.
   - **Where to Find It**: There are specialty jewelry shops in **World Bazaar** (Tokyo Disneyland) and **American Waterfront** (Tokyo DisneySea).

Best Souvenirs for Each Type of Visitor

1. **For Families**
   - **Stuffed Animals and Plush Toys**: These are perfect for kids and adults! Choose from iconic Disney characters like Mickey and Minnie or more recent favorites like the characters from *Frozen* and *Toy Story*.
   - **Where to Find It**: You can find plush toys at almost every store, but the best selection is at **the Merchandise Shops** near the entrances of both parks.

- **Must-Try**: The **Mickey and Minnie plush set** or a **Duffy and Friends** plushie from DisneySea.

2. **For Couples**

    - **Themed Dining Sets**: A romantic way to bring home Disney magic. You can purchase **Mickey or Minnie-themed dinnerware**, from plates and mugs to teacups and serving dishes.

    - **Where to Find It**: Look for high-quality Disney merchandise at stores like **The Crystal Palace** and **Disney's Boutique** in Disneyland.

    - **Must-Try**: A **Mickey Mouse-shaped tea set** or a **Minnie Mouse-themed mug**.

3. **For Solo Travelers**

    - **Disney Art and Prints**: For solo travelers, something unique like Disney artwork or print might be the perfect souvenir. You can find beautiful prints of iconic Disney scenes and characters and limited-edition art prints that will remind you of your magical adventure.

    - **Where to Find It**: Head to the **Art Gallery** at **Disney Gallery** in **World Bazaar** (Tokyo Disneyland) or the **Mediterranean Harbor** in **DisneySea**.

    - **Must-Try**: A limited-edition **DisneySea artwork** or **Cinderella Castle print**.

Hidden Shopping Spots

Now, let's talk about **hidden shopping spots**—those little-known shops tucked away in corners of the parks that offer unique and exclusive finds. These places are where the true Disney treasure hunters can score the most sought-after items!

Lesser-Known Shops for Unique Finds

1. **Lost River Delta Shops (Tokyo DisneySea)**
   - **Why It's a Hidden Gem**: Located in the **Lost River Delta**, this area has several small shops filled with jungle-themed and adventure-inspired merchandise. It's not crowded, making it a peaceful place to shop and discover unique souvenirs that you won't find anywhere else.
   - **Must-Have Items**:
     - **Indiana Jones-inspired merchandise**, like hats and bags.
     - **Exotic treasures** like handcrafted jewelry and art inspired by the jungles.
2. **Gag Factory (Tokyo Disneyland)**
   - **Why It's a Hidden Gem**: Located near ToonTown, this quirky store offers

82 |TOKYO DISNEY RESORT

novelty items and fun, offbeat Disney products.

- **Must-Have Items**:
- **Gag gifts**, like funny hats, novelty keychains, and Disney-themed toys.
- **Mickey Mouse-themed puzzles** and games for family fun.

3. **The Tower of Terror Shop (Tokyo DisneySea)**
   - **Why It's a Hidden Gem**: Hidden in the **American Waterfront** near the Tower of Terror, this shop is easy to miss but offers exclusive, eerie-themed souvenirs that tie into the ride.
   - **Must-Have Items**:
   - **Spooky-themed merchandise** such as haunted house accessories, eerie artwork, and exclusive Tower of Terror souvenirs.
   - **Vintage-style luggage** and **travel items** with a mysterious, haunted vibe.

Secret Souvenirs Only Disney Fans Will Know

1. **Vintage Mickey Collectibles**
   - **Where to Find It**: Vintage **Mickey Mouse collectibles** are often hidden in

obscure stores like **The Crystal Palace** throughout the park.

- **What Makes It Special**: These items often feature the older versions of Mickey and Minnie, adding a unique retro touch to your Disney collection.

2. **Duffy and Friends**

    - **Where to Find It**: Available primarily in **Tokyo DisneySea**, Duffy and his friends have a massive cult following, and their merchandise is often exclusive to the park.

    - **What Makes It Special**: If you're a fan of Duffy, ShellieMay, Gelatoni, or CookieAnn, this is the perfect souvenir to take home. Look for exclusive **Duffy Plushes**, **costumes**, and **accessories**.

Hidden Gems and Lesser-Known Spots

Tokyo Disney Resort is full of well-known attractions, parades, and beloved characters, but if you look closely, you'll discover a world of **hidden gems** waiting to be explored. These secret spots, quieter areas, and underrated experiences offer a chance to immerse yourself in the magic without the crowds. This is your insider's guide to the lesser-known wonders that make Tokyo Disney Resort even more magical.

Secret Areas to Explore

Tokyo Disney Resort is filled with spots that many visitors overlook. These are places where you can relax, snap a perfect photo, or enjoy a peaceful moment away from the crowds. These areas might not be on the usual maps, but they are worth seeking.

Quiet Spots for Relaxing and Photos

1. **Tom Sawyer Island (Tokyo Disneyland)**
    - **Why It's Special**: Tom Sawyer Island is a secluded part of Tokyo Disneyland that feels like a world of its own. Accessible only by raft, it offers quiet walking paths, little nooks to rest, and stunning views of the riverside and **Cinderella Castle**.

- **What to Do**: Stroll around the island, take in the lush, tranquil scenery, and enjoy the beautiful views of the park from a distance. This is a perfect spot to relax, take photos, and escape the hustle and bustle of the main areas.

- **Insider Tip**: Look for the **secret caves** and hidden passages. These little features make the island feel like a genuine adventure.

2. **The Secret Garden (Tokyo Disneyland)**

    - **Why It's Special**: Near **Fantasyland**, there is a quiet, hidden garden that most visitors miss. The Secret Garden is a lush, tranquil spot perfect for taking a peaceful break.

    - **What to Do**: Wander through this tucked-away paradise, enjoy the flowers, and sit by the fountain to relax. It's one of the park's hidden oases, where you can unwind and escape the crowds.

    - **Insider Tip**: The garden is not well-marked, so it can be tricky to find. Take a moment to pause and look for the winding paths leading to this peaceful retreat.

3. **Mediterranean Harbor (Tokyo DisneySea)**

    - **Why It's Special**: Although this area of DisneySea is stunning, many visitors don't fully appreciate its quieter spots. The

Mediterranean Harbor offers beautiful vistas, serene walking paths, and hidden corners, perfect for a relaxing break or a romantic moment.

- **What to Do**: Head towards the quieter side of the harbor for a calm stroll or to capture stunning photographs of the harbor and **Tower of Terror** in the distance. There are fewer crowds here, making it perfect for those seeking peace and inspiration.

- **Insider Tip**: Look for small **hidden cafes** along the way that offer peaceful spots to sit and enjoy the atmosphere without the large crowds.

4. **The Enchanted Tiki Room (Tokyo Disneyland)**

    - **Why It's Special**: While not technically a "hidden" spot, this attraction offers a much-needed escape from the sun and crowds. Located in **Adventureland**, the Enchanted Tiki Room provides a relaxing, air-conditioned retreat with colorful animatronic birds singing tropical tunes.

    - **What to Do**: Sit back and enjoy the show, take in the lush tropical setting, and listen to the peaceful sounds of the jungle. It's a perfect spot to recharge when you need a break from the more thrilling rides.

    - **Insider Tip**: Don't rush through this one—truly enjoy the atmosphere and the calming tropical setting.

Hidden-Themed Areas You May Miss

1. **Arabian Coast (Tokyo DisneySea)**
   - **Why It's Special**: Located on the far side of DisneySea, the **Arabian Coast** is often overlooked, yet it's full of hidden gems. Inspired by the tales of *Aladdin*, this area features Arabian-themed shops, restaurants, and attractions.
   - **What to Do**: Explore the winding streets, discover the intricately detailed buildings, and visit **Sindbad's Storybook Voyage**, one of the park's most charming attractions. The shops are often less crowded than in other parts of the park and sell unique DisneySea merchandise.
   - **Insider Tip**: Look for **secret items** in the stores, such as limited-edition **Aladdin-themed collectibles** or **specialty spices** that reflect the region's exotic feel.

2. **The American Waterfront (Tokyo DisneySea)**
   - **Why It's Special**: The **American Waterfront** is one of the largest areas in DisneySea, but it hides some of the best spots that many visitors walk past without noticing. From the charming **New York street** to the beautiful **Cape Cod area**, the waterfront offers a variety of experiences.

- **What to Do**: Take a stroll down **New York Street**, where you can admire the details of the architecture and discover hidden boutiques. The quieter, charming **Cape Cod** area is perfect for a romantic walk and offers stunning views of **S.S. Columbia**.

- **Insider Tip**: Look for **hidden dining spots** like **Dockside Diner**, which offers a peaceful ambiance and a perfect spot to watch the **"Fantasmic!"** show from the shore.

3. **Lost River Delta (Tokyo DisneySea)**

   - **Why It's Special**: Often missed by visitors rushing to the more famous attractions, the **Lost River Delta** in DisneySea offers a hidden park corner with jungle vibes and adventure-filled experiences.

   - **What to Do**: Explore the **Indiana Jones Adventure: Temple of the Crystal Skull** and stroll through the jungle. Plenty of hidden details in the décor, including ancient ruins and secret passages, make this area feel genuinely immersive.

   - **Insider Tip**: Venture more deeply into the area to find the **secret caves** and spots where you can relax and listen to the sounds of the jungle.

Underrated Attractions

Tokyo Disney Resort is full of world-class attractions, but some don't always get the spotlight, yet they offer just as much fun, excitement, and magic. Here are a few **underrated attractions** that are definitely worth your time:

1. **The Many Adventures of Winnie the Pooh (Tokyo Disneyland)**

    - **Why It's Underrated**: Although this ride is a fan favorite, it overshadows other significant popular attractions. It offers a whimsical, trackless ride that brings you through the pages of the beloved Pooh stories.

    - **What to Do**: Take a ride through **Pooh's Hunny Hunt**, where you'll experience charming scenes and hidden surprises that make the attraction magical.

    - **Insider Tip**: Look for the **Honey Hunt scenes** and interact with the "honey pots" along the ride. It's not just a ride—it's a magical journey into the heart of Winnie the Pooh's world.

2. **The Little Mermaid: Ariel's Undersea Adventure (Tokyo DisneySea)**

    - **Why It's Underrated**: Although the ride is one of the quieter attractions in **Mermaid Lagoon**, it's beautifully themed and charming. It doesn't always get the attention of other thrilling rides, but it offers a peaceful and immersive experience.

- **What to Do**: Sit back and enjoy the journey under the sea, with scenes that recreate the most memorable moments from *The Little Mermaid*. The ride's gentle pace and captivating visuals make it perfect for all ages.
- **Insider Tip**: Pay attention to the tiny details in the ride's set design—hidden secrets are tucked into each scene that true Disney fans will appreciate.

3. **Monsters, Inc. Ride & Go Seek (Tokyo Disneyland)**
    - **Why It's Underrated**: While this interactive ride is loved by those who know about it, it often gets overshadowed by the larger thrill rides in the park. It offers an entirely different experience, where guests use flashlights to "find" monsters hidden throughout the ride.
    - **What to Do**: Hunt for monsters and interact with the interactive elements throughout the ride. It's a fun, playful experience perfect for families with children but offers a quirky, surprising adventure for adults.
    - **Insider Tip**: Don't be afraid to shine your flashlight on everything—hidden monsters are waiting for you to discover, making the experience unique each time.

Off-the-Beaten-Path Experiences

Tokyo Disney Resort isn't just about the famous rides and attractions; plenty of **unique experiences** take you off the beaten path. These activities let you explore hidden corners of the parks and enjoy special moments that most visitors might miss.

1. **Themed Dining Experiences**
   - **Why It's Off-the-Beaten-Path**: While character dining is well-known, a few **themed dining experiences** often fly under the radar. For example, dining at **Magellan's** in DisneySea offers an excellent meal and an immersive atmosphere.
   - **What to Do**: Enjoy a fine dining experience in an exclusive setting, where you'll feel part of a secret adventure. The restaurant's story is tied to explorations and discoveries, making it a dining experience with a twist.
   - **Insider Tip**: Book your reservations early—these spots are often more challenging to get into, and you don't want to miss out on the chance to dine in style.

2. **Duffy & Friends Meet-and-Greet (Tokyo DisneySea)**
   - **Why It's Off-the-Beaten-Path**: While **Mickey Mouse** and **Goofy** are the most

famous characters to meet, **Duffy & Friends** are beloved by many Disney fans, especially those who know the more profound lore of Tokyo DisneySea. These cuddly characters have their own dedicated space in DisneySea.

- **What to Do**: Find **Duffy, ShellieMay, Gelatoni**, and **CookieAnn** in the **American Waterfront** area for a fun, low-key meet-and-greet. These characters aren't always on the typical character meet-and-greet paths, making the experience more exclusive.

- **Insider Tip**: If you're a fan of Duffy and his friends, be sure to visit their official shop, where you'll find exclusive merchandise not available in other parts of the park.

3. **Tokyo Disneyland Electrical Parade Dreamlights (Tokyo Disneyland)**

    - **Why It's Off-the-Beaten-Path**: While this parade is a classic, many visitors overlook the unique spots around the park that offer great views without the crowded areas by the main parade route.

    - **What to Do**: For a less crowded experience, head to **the World Bazaar** or areas around **Cinderella Castle**. Enjoy the dazzling lights and magical floats as the park lights up for the parade.

    - **Insider Tip**: If you can, find a spot near the **Castle Forecourt** for a prime view. You'll be able to see the magical floats without being packed in with large crowds.

Exclusive Experiences

Tokyo Disney Resort is a world of magic, but for those looking to experience it in a way that's truly extraordinary, there's a whole other level of enchantment waiting to be discovered. From VIP tours that offer behind-the-scenes access to exclusive meet-and-greets with Disney characters, these luxurious experiences are designed to make you feel like royalty. Whether you're seeking a private tour, the best seats in the house for a parade, or the chance to meet rare Disney characters, there's an experience at Tokyo Disney Resort that will surpass your wildest dreams. Let's dive into the world of **exclusive experiences** that will make your time at the resort even more unforgettable.

VIP Tours and Special Access

Imagine bypassing the lines, having your own personal guide, and enjoying the magic of Disney like a true VIP. Tokyo Disney Resort offers exclusive tours that elevate your visit into something truly special. With access to behind-the-scenes areas, early access to attractions, and tailored experiences, you'll feel like you've stepped into a world designed just for you.

How to Book VIP Tours and Behind-the-Scenes Experiences

1. **Booking the VIP Tour**

- **How to Book**: VIP Tours at Tokyo Disney Resort are available through the official resort website, where you can choose from a variety of tour options depending on your needs. You can also book through your hotel concierge if you're staying at one of the Disney Resort Hotels, which is a recommended route for ease.

- **VIP Tour Types**:
    - **Private VIP Tours**: These allow you to explore the park with your own personal guide, customizing the experience based on your interests. Whether you want to focus on thrill rides, character meet-and-greets, or enjoying exclusive shows, the guide will tailor the experience to suit your desires.
    - **Behind-the-Scenes Tours**: These tours give you access to areas of the park that most guests never see. From the inner workings of the attractions to special areas like **Cast Member-only zones**, this is the ultimate way to experience the magic of Disney in a way that very few ever do.

2. **Costs and Availability**
    - **Cost**: Prices for VIP Tours typically start at around **¥100,000–¥150,000** per day, depending on the length of the tour and the level of exclusivity. While these experiences are on the higher end of the

budget, the memories and personalized service are priceless.

- **Booking in Advance**: VIP tours are highly sought after, so be sure to book as early as possible to secure your spot, especially during peak seasons like holidays and special events. **Availability** is limited, and tours may be subject to availability due to the resort's schedule.

3. **What to Expect from a VIP Tour**

    - **Personalized Experience**: Your tour guide will take you through both Tokyo Disneyland and Tokyo DisneySea, skipping the lines and providing exclusive access to attractions and shows. You'll also receive priority seating for parades and shows.

    - **Exclusive Access**: Enjoy behind-the-scenes looks at your favorite attractions and characters, private meet-and-greets, and access to VIP-only areas in the park.

    - **Tailored Itinerary**: Whether you're focused on thrilling rides or exploring the artistic side of Disney, your tour guide will customize the experience to make sure it matches your interests.

Exclusive Access to Rides, Shows, and Events

VIP experiences at Tokyo Disney Resort aren't just about avoiding the crowds—they offer exclusive access to the most sought-after rides, shows, and events.

1. **Early Access to Attractions**
   - Skip the lines for the most popular rides, including **Space Mountain**, **Big Thunder Mountain**, and **Journey to the Center of the Earth**. With VIP access, you can bypass long wait times, giving you more time to enjoy the magic of the park.
   - **Must-See VIP Perks**: VIP guests often receive early access to newly opened attractions or special seasonal events before they are available to the general public. For example, in 2025, VIP guests may have the opportunity to enjoy special **Frozen-themed experiences** before they are fully released.

2. **Exclusive Access to Shows and Events**
   - **Priority Seating for Parades and Fireworks**: VIP guests enjoy exclusive seating for some of the park's most popular shows and parades. From the dazzling **"Dreaming Up!" Parade** at Tokyo Disneyland to the majestic **Fantasmic!** at Tokyo DisneySea, VIP guests will be treated to the best seats in the house.

- **Behind-the-Scenes Shows**: Some tours even offer the opportunity to watch live performances from backstage or enjoy special, private performances that are not available to general guests. These are **exclusive opportunities** for those looking to experience Disney in a truly unique way.

Character Meet-and-Greets

Meeting Disney characters is one of the most magical experiences at Tokyo Disney Resort. However, for those who want a more exclusive, intimate interaction, there are **VIP character meet-and-greets** that offer personalized moments with your favorite characters.

Best Times and Locations to Meet Your Favorite Characters

1. **Location: Mickey's Toontown (Tokyo Disneyland)**
   - **Why It's Special**: Mickey's Toontown is home to the iconic **Mickey Mouse** and **Minnie Mouse** houses, where you can meet these famous characters in a peaceful, fun setting. While there is always a line for Mickey, **VIP access** lets you bypass the queue for a private meet-and-greet.
   - **Best Time**: Early morning or later in the evening, right before the park closes, to avoid larger crowds.

2. **Location: DisneySea's Mediterranean Harbor (Tokyo DisneySea)**

    - **Why It's Special**: This area is home to some of the park's rarer characters, such as **Duffy and Friends**. These lovable characters have their own special meet-and-greet area that's often less crowded, making it ideal for a more intimate experience.

    - **Best Time**: Afternoon hours, when the crowds tend to thin out. VIP access allows for private photos and autographs without the usual long waits.

3. **Character Dining**

    - **Why It's Special**: For an even more personal experience, character dining is a wonderful way to meet Disney characters in a relaxed, sit-down setting. Enjoy a meal while characters like **Goofy**, **Donald Duck**, and **Pluto** visit your table for photos and interactions.

    - **Where to Find It: Chef Mickey** (Disney Ambassador Hotel) and **Plaza Restaurant** (Tokyo Disneyland) offer some of the best character dining experiences.

    - **Best Time**: Book a reservation for lunch or dinner during off-peak hours to avoid long wait times and ensure the best experience.

Rare and Exclusive Character Appearances

For those who seek something truly unique, Tokyo Disney Resort offers rare character meet-and-greets that are exclusive to VIPs and those who know where to look.

1. **VIP Character Meet-and-Greets**
   - **Why It's Special**: Some characters are hidden away in exclusive locations where only VIP guests can meet them. For instance, the elusive **Princesses** like **Ariel**, **Belle**, and **Rapunzel** often have private meet-and-greets that can be arranged through your VIP tour package.
   - **Insider Tip**: Ask your VIP guide about character meet-and-greets that aren't on the regular schedules. They can often provide access to rare appearances that aren't publicly announced.

2. **Seasonal or Themed Character Events**
   - **Why It's Special**: Certain times of the year offer the chance to meet **seasonal characters** or special character outfits that are exclusive to events such as Halloween or Christmas. In 2025, look out for limited-edition meet-and-greet opportunities during the **40th Anniversary celebrations**.

- **Insider Tip**: These appearances often happen in less crowded areas or at times when the park is quieter, making it a great opportunity for photos and memories.

Seasonal Events and Festivals in 2025

Tokyo Disney Resort is known for its seasonal events and celebrations that transform the parks into an entirely new experience. From dazzling shows to exclusive merchandise and seasonal treats, 2025 is set to bring even more magic to these events.

Limited-Time Events and Shows at Tokyo Disney Resort

1. 40th Anniversary Celebration (2025)
    - **Why It's Special**: In 2025, Tokyo Disney Resort celebrates its **40th Anniversary** with an entire year of special events, parades, and limited-edition merchandise. This milestone celebration will bring exclusive shows, limited-time attractions, and special character appearances.
    - **What to Expect**: Special performances, including **new parade floats**, anniversary-themed dining experiences,

and unique shows celebrating the resort's 40-year legacy.

- **Exclusive Access**: VIPs may receive **early access** to certain anniversary events, including backstage tours and special access to themed celebrations.

2. **Halloween and Christmas Events**

    - **Why It's Special**: Halloween and Christmas at Tokyo Disney Resort are renowned for their immersive decorations, themed parades, and seasonal treats. In 2025, these celebrations will be bigger and more exclusive than ever.

    - **What to Expect**: Expect dazzling decorations at both parks, exclusive seasonal merchandise, and themed shows and parades. **VIP tours** may also offer special behind-the-scenes access to the creation of these seasonal displays.

    - **Insider Tip**: During Halloween and Christmas, the park offers exclusive **limited-edition character merchandise**, as well as seasonal food and drinks that will only be available for a short period.

3. **Disneyland's Dreaming Up Parade (2025)**

    - **Why It's Special**: This spectacular parade combines stunning floats, beloved Disney characters, and vibrant music. In 2025, the **Dreaming Up! Parade** will feature exclusive, never-before-seen elements to mark the anniversary.

- **Exclusive Access**: VIPs will enjoy **reserved viewing areas** with the best spots for photos and unobstructed views of the parade.

Itineraries

Planning your perfect day at **Tokyo Disney Resort** can be overwhelming with so many attractions, shows, and experiences to choose from. Don't worry—I've got you covered! Whether you're visiting with family, as a couple, or traveling solo, this section provides **custom itineraries** to ensure you make the most of your time. Each itinerary is designed with your specific needs in mind, so you can maximize your visit while still having time to enjoy the magic.

1-Day Itinerary for Families, Couples, and Solo Travelers

When you have just one day at **Tokyo Disney Resort**, you want to make it count. Here are three tailored itineraries to help you have an unforgettable experience in just one day.

A Perfect Day for Families

A day at Tokyo Disney Resort with kids should be filled with fun, adventure, and plenty of character encounters. Here's how to make the most of your time together.

1. **Morning**:
    - **Arrive Early**: Aim to arrive right when the park opens to make the most of the quieter morning hours.

- **Head to Fantasyland**: Start your day with classic family attractions like **"It's a Small World"** and **Pooh's Hunny Hunt**. These are perfect for kids and offer gentle fun without long wait times early in the day.

- **Must-Do Character Meet-and-Greet**: Head to **Mickey's Toontown** for a chance to meet Mickey and Minnie. This area is less crowded in the morning, making it perfect for a family photo with your favorite characters.

2. **Midday**:

    - **Lunch at Plaza Restaurant**: Enjoy a relaxing character dining experience at the **Plaza Restaurant**. It's a buffet-style meal with popular Disney characters, and it's a great way to recharge for the afternoon.

    - **Pirates of the Caribbean**: After lunch, take the family on a thrilling yet kid-friendly ride through the pirate world. It's a must-see attraction that offers immersive storytelling and cool special effects.

3. **Afternoon**:

    - **Big Thunder Mountain**: As the crowds start to build, head to **Big Thunder Mountain**. It's a fun roller coaster that will excite older kids and adults in the family.

- **Take a Break at Tom Sawyer Island**: After some thrills, relax on Tom Sawyer Island. It's a quiet escape where you can take a stroll and let the kids explore hidden caves and tunnels.

4. **Evening**:

    - **Dinner at the Hungry Bear Restaurant**: For a laid-back, family-friendly meal, enjoy burgers and fried chicken at **Hungry Bear** in **Westernland**. This spot is great for families and offers a cozy, rustic atmosphere.
    - **End with the Dreaming Up! Parade**: Secure a good spot along the parade route and enjoy the vibrant, magical **Dreaming Up! Parade**, featuring Disney characters and colorful floats. It's a spectacular way to end a fun-filled family day.

A Romantic Day for Couples

For couples, Tokyo Disney Resort offers plenty of romantic and relaxing experiences amidst all the magic. Here's how to enjoy a romantic day together.

1. **Morning**:

    - **Start with Breakfast at Disney Ambassador Hotel**: Begin your day with a relaxed breakfast at the **Disney Ambassador Hotel**. The hotel has a luxurious atmosphere, and the breakfast options are perfect to start your day in style.

- **Head to Tokyo DisneySea**: DisneySea offers a more romantic, serene atmosphere with its European and Mediterranean themes. Start by exploring **Mediterranean Harbor**, where you can take a boat ride and enjoy stunning views of the park.

- **Enjoy a Relaxing Ride on Venetian Gondolas**: Share a peaceful moment on the **Venetian gondola ride** in DisneySea's **Mediterranean Harbor**. It's an intimate and picturesque experience that's perfect for couples.

2. **Midday**:

- **Lunch at Magellan's**: For an upscale, romantic dining experience, book a table at **Magellan's** in **Mysterious Island**. This fine-dining restaurant offers Mediterranean cuisine in an opulent, explorer-themed setting.

- **Explore the Arabian Coast**: After lunch, stroll through the **Arabian Coast**, which has a beautiful, intimate atmosphere. Visit the small shops, enjoy the intricate details of the architecture, and take in the ambiance.

3. **Afternoon**:
   - **Take in the Tower of Terror**: For a thrilling yet not-too-scary adventure, visit the **Tower of Terror** in DisneySea. This attraction offers an exciting mix of chills and thrills, perfect for couples looking for a little excitement.
   - **Visit the American Waterfront**: End your afternoon exploring the **American Waterfront** area. Enjoy a leisurely walk around the beautiful waterfront and visit the shops for unique DisneySea-themed souvenirs.

4. **Evening**:
   - **Dinner at the S.S. Columbia Dining Room**: For a romantic dinner, enjoy a meal at the **S.S. Columbia Dining Room** in **American Waterfront**. This upscale restaurant offers American cuisine with fantastic views of the harbor.
   - **Watch Fantasmic!**: End your day with the magical **Fantasmic!** show, which combines fireworks, water projections, and Disney characters. Watch it from the best VIP seating area, reserved for those seeking the most exclusive experience.

Solo Traveler's Guide to Tokyo Disney Resort

Solo travelers can enjoy a flexible, exciting experience at Tokyo Disney Resort, without having to worry about making plans for others. Here's a day designed to give you the most out of your solo adventure.

1. **Morning**:
    - **Arrive Early**: Get to the park when it opens for a peaceful start to the day before the crowds build.
    - **Start with Space Mountain**: Head straight to **Space Mountain** for an adrenaline-pumping solo adventure. The first few hours are perfect for hitting the rides with the shortest lines.
    - **Explore Tomorrowland**: Take some time to explore **Tomorrowland**, with attractions like **Star Tours** and **Monsters, Inc. Ride & Go Seek**, both of which are interactive and fun solo experiences.
2. **Midday**:
    - **Solo Dining at Hokusai**: For lunch, enjoy a serene meal at **Hokusai** in the Tokyo Disneyland Hotel. This upscale Japanese restaurant is perfect for solo travelers who want to enjoy fine dining in a peaceful environment.

- **Stroll Through Fantasyland**: After lunch, head to **Fantasyland** and take a slow stroll through the enchanting areas. Spend time on **It's a Small World** and **Pooh's Hunny Hunt**, perfect for relaxing and enjoying the charm of Disney without rushing.

3. **Afternoon**:

   - **Take in the Jungle Cruise**: For a fun solo experience, embark on the **Jungle Cruise**. This lighthearted, interactive boat ride is a great way to experience the park's humor and tropical vibes while meeting other solo travelers.

   - **Visit the Enchanted Tiki Room**: For a more laid-back experience, head to the **Enchanted Tiki Room**. Relax in the cool air-conditioned space and enjoy the tropical birds' delightful performances.

4. **Evening**:

   - **Dinner at Ristorante di Canaletto**: Solo travelers will appreciate the quiet and relaxing atmosphere of **Ristorante di Canaletto**. Located in **Mediterranean Harbor**, this restaurant offers beautiful views and authentic Italian cuisine, perfect for winding down after a busy day.

   - **Catch the Dreaming Up! Parade**: Finish your day by watching the **Dreaming Up! Parade**. The beauty of solo travel is that you can stand exactly where you want for the best view of the parade, capturing the magical moment.

Multiple-Day Itinerary

If you're planning a longer visit to Tokyo Disney Resort, you have the opportunity to explore even more of the magic. Here's how to make the most of a **3-day**, **5-day**, and **7-day** stay.

3-Day Itinerary: Making the Most of Your Time

For those with a bit more time, here's how to maximize your three days at the resort.

1. **Day 1: Tokyo Disneyland**

    - **Morning**: Start your day with classic attractions like **Pirates of the Caribbean, Big Thunder Mountain**, and **Splash Mountain**. These iconic rides are a must for first-time visitors.

    - **Afternoon**: Explore **Fantasyland** and visit **It's a Small World, Pooh's Hunny Hunt**, and **The Many Adventures of Winnie the Pooh**. For lunch, dine at **Plaza Restaurant** for a character dining experience.

    - **Evening**: End your day with the **Dreaming Up! Parade** and enjoy dinner at **The Crystal Palace**.

Afterward, take a peaceful stroll through **World Bazaar**.

2. **Day 2: Tokyo DisneySea**

    - **Morning**: Start your day in **Mediterranean Harbor** and enjoy **Venetian Gondolas** and **Sinbad's Storybook Voyage**.

    - **Afternoon**: Head to **Mysterious Island** and experience **Journey to the Center of the Earth** and **20,000 Leagues Under the Sea**. Don't miss **Indiana Jones Adventure** in **Lost River Delta**.

    - **Evening**: Watch **Fantasmic!** and enjoy a romantic dinner at **Magellan's**.

3. **Day 3: Explore More and Catch Seasonal Events**

    - **Morning**: Revisit your favorite attractions from Day 1, like **Space Mountain** and **Splash Mountain**. Check out any seasonal events, such as special parades or character meet-and-greets.

    - **Afternoon**: Explore **American Waterfront** and visit **S.S. Columbia** for lunch. Enjoy some quiet time in **Arabian Coast**.

    - **Evening**: Head back to **Fantasyland** for a peaceful evening and catch a late performance of **Dreaming Up! Parade**.

5-Day Itinerary: Exploring Every Corner of the Resort

With five days, you can take a more leisurely pace and experience the full breadth of the resort.

1. **Day 1-2**: Focus on Tokyo Disneyland and Tokyo DisneySea as outlined in the 3-day itinerary. Use Day 1 for **Tokyo Disneyland** and Day 2 for **Tokyo DisneySea**.

2. **Day 3: Shopping and Relaxation**
   - Spend your third day exploring hidden shops, indulging in exclusive dining experiences, and taking in shows. Visit areas like **Mickey's Toontown** for a more relaxed vibe and enjoy an afternoon of shopping.

3. **Day 4: Day Trip or Exclusive VIP Tour**
   - Consider booking a **VIP tour** for behind-the-scenes access to attractions or a **private guide** for personalized experiences.
   - Alternatively, use the day to explore nearby attractions outside the resort, such as a trip to **Maihama** or **Odaiba**.

4. **Day 5: Revisit Favorites and Enjoy Seasonal Events**
    - Use this final day to revisit your favorite attractions, take in any seasonal events you might have missed, and relax before you head home.

7-Day Itinerary: Extended Stay with Day Trips

A full week gives you ample time to explore every corner of Tokyo Disney Resort and venture outside the resort for day trips.

1. **Day 1-3**: Follow the 5-day itinerary, allowing you to fully experience Tokyo Disneyland and Tokyo DisneySea, and then enjoy shopping, relaxation, and VIP tours.

2. **Day 4: Explore Outside the Resort**
    - Take a **day trip to Tokyo**: Visit **Odaiba**, explore **Ginza**, or check out the **Meiji Shrine**. These places offer a nice balance of culture, shopping, and relaxation.

3. **Day 5-6**: Revisit your favorite spots in both parks, attend seasonal events, and enjoy any exclusive experiences, like VIP meet-and-greets or private tours.

4. **Day 7**: Wrap up your trip by enjoying a final day of leisure, shopping, and taking in the sights and sounds of the resort.

Rides and Shows to Prioritize

With so many options available, it's crucial to prioritize the best attractions and shows to ensure you don't miss out on the must-do experiences.

Which Attractions You Can't Miss

- **Space Mountain**: A classic ride in **Tomorrowland**, perfect for thrill-seekers.

- **Pirates of the Caribbean**: An immersive boat ride in **Adventureland**, filled with storytelling and special effects.

- **Journey to the Center of the Earth**: A thrilling ride in **Mysterious Island** at DisneySea.

How to Avoid the Long Lines

- **Arrive Early**: Get to the parks before they open to enjoy popular attractions with shorter wait times.

- **Use FastPass**: Make sure to take advantage of the **FastPass** system for high-demand rides, which allows you to bypass the regular lines and enjoy other attractions while you wait for your designated time.

- **Visit During Off-Peak Times**: Weekdays, especially Tuesday to Thursday, are usually less crowded.

Tips and Tricks for a Magical Experience

Tokyo Disney Resort is a magical place, and making the most of your visit can make the difference between a good time and an unforgettable one. There's no shortage of fun, but with a little insider knowledge, you can maximize your time, beat the crowds, and ensure you're prepared for everything the resort has to offer. Let me share some practical tips and tricks that will help you make the most of your day and create lasting memories.

Maximizing Your Time

With so much to see and do at Tokyo Disney Resort, time is your most precious resource. Here are some tips to help you make the most of your time and enjoy a stress-free day in the parks.

Using the Tokyo Disney Resort App

1. **Download the Official App**
   - **Why It's Essential**: The **Tokyo Disney Resort App** is a game-changer. It's free to download and offers a wealth of information at your fingertips. From ride wait times and show schedules to mobile food ordering and interactive

maps, the app is your ultimate guide to the resort.

- **What It Can Do**:
    - **Ride Wait Times**: Keep track of current wait times for rides in real time. This allows you to make smart decisions on which attractions to visit next.
    - **Mobile Food Ordering**: Save time by ordering food in advance at select restaurants. You'll skip the lines and enjoy more time exploring.
    - **Maps and Directions**: Use the app's interactive maps to navigate the parks, find restroom locations, and locate your favorite shops and attractions.

2. **Notifications and Updates**
    - Turn on **notifications** for real-time updates about any changes in show schedules, ride closures, or special offers. This feature will keep you in the know, so you don't miss out on anything exciting.

Best Strategies for Beating the Lines

Long waits can eat into your fun, but with the right strategy, you can minimize your time in lines and make the most of every moment.

1. **Arrive Early**
   - **Why It Works**: Arriving before the park officially opens, often referred to as **"rope drop"**, gives you the chance to experience some of the most popular rides before the crowds arrive.
   - **What to Do**: Head straight to the major attractions like **Space Mountain** or **Splash Mountain** when the park opens, and you'll get to enjoy them with shorter wait times.

2. **Head to Popular Rides First**
   - **Why It Works**: Attractions like **Pirates of the Caribbean, Big Thunder Mountain**, and **Journey to the Center of the Earth** are major crowd-pleasers. Visit these first thing in the morning to avoid the midday crowds.

3. **Strategically Time Your Visits**
   - **What to Do**: Ride **thrill rides** early in the morning and save gentler rides, like **It's a Small World**, for the later afternoon when lines tend to be shorter. Shows and parades also have peak and off-peak times, so plan accordingly.

FastPass and Queue Management Tips

1. **Use FastPass for Popular Rides**
   - **How It Works**: The FastPass system allows you to reserve access to certain attractions ahead of time, skipping the standard queue. Simply head to the designated FastPass distribution points in the parks and pick your preferred time slot.
   - **Best Attractions for FastPass**:
     - **Big Thunder Mountain**
     - **Space Mountain**
     - **Indiana Jones Adventure**
     - **Splash Mountain**
   - **Pro Tip**: Be strategic with your FastPasses! Once you've used your first one, head straight to another attraction for your next FastPass. You can book another after you've redeemed your previous FastPass.

2. **Single Rider Lines**
   - **Why It's Helpful**: If you're traveling solo or don't mind riding separately from your group, take advantage of **Single Rider Lines**. These are often shorter

and can save you a significant amount of time.

- **Where to Use It**: Popular attractions like **Splash Mountain** and **Big Thunder Mountain** often have Single Rider Lines that move faster.

Dealing with Crowds

Tokyo Disney Resort can get crowded, especially during peak times. But don't worry! With a few smart moves, you can dodge the crowds and still enjoy a fun-filled day.

When to Visit Specific Attractions to Avoid the Crowds

1. **Early Morning and Late Afternoon**

    - **Why It Works**: The parks are generally less crowded during the first few hours after opening and in the late afternoon as people start to head out. Take advantage of these times to visit popular attractions that have long wait times during midday.

    - **Pro Tip**: If you're visiting during peak seasons, try visiting attractions near the back of the park early in the day (such as **Tomorrowland** in Disneyland) and work your way toward the front.

2. **Check Show Times**
   - **Why It Works**: During peak parade and show times, many guests flock to the parades and shows, leaving the rides less crowded. Plan to visit attractions during these moments for shorter lines.
   - **Pro Tip**: While everyone is watching the **Dreaming Up! Parade**, head to popular rides like **Splash Mountain** or **Space Mountain** for significantly shorter wait times.

3. **Avoid the Midday Rush**
   - **What to Do**: During midday, especially between 11 a.m. and 2 p.m., the parks tend to be the most crowded. This is a great time to take a break, enjoy lunch, or visit indoor attractions and shows that have lower wait times.

Off-Peak Hours for Maximum Enjoyment

1. **Weekdays Are Your Friend**
   - **Why It Works**: Weekdays, particularly Tuesdays through Thursdays, are less crowded than weekends. If you can plan your visit for these days, you'll avoid the weekend rush and have a more relaxed experience.

- **Pro Tip**: If your schedule allows, try to visit during off-peak seasons like **mid-January to mid-February** or **mid-May to June** when there are fewer guests and shorter lines.

2. **Take Advantage of Evening Hours**
   - **Why It Works**: As the sun sets, many families with younger children start heading home, and the parks become quieter. You can enjoy the attractions with shorter wait times and catch some of the special **nighttime shows** like **Fantasmic!** and **the Electrical Parade**.
   - **Pro Tip**: The **last hour** of the park's operation can be one of the best times to visit rides with long wait times earlier in the day.

Packing Essentials

Packing for Tokyo Disney Resort might seem straightforward, but there are a few key essentials you'll need to ensure your day goes smoothly. Here's a guide to help you pack efficiently.

What to Bring and What to Leave Behind

1. **What to Bring:**
   - **Comfortable Shoes**: You'll be walking a lot, so make sure to bring **comfortable, broken-in shoes** that can handle a full day of walking. Sneakers or supportive sandals are ideal.
   - **Portable Battery Charger**: The Tokyo Disney Resort app, photos, and videos can drain your phone's battery quickly. A portable charger will keep you connected and allow you to use the app throughout the day.
   - **Water Bottle**: Hydration is key, especially on hot days. While you can purchase drinks in the parks, bring an empty water bottle that you can refill at water fountains throughout the resort.
   - **Sunscreen and Hat**: If you're visiting during the warmer months, sunscreen is essential, as are sunglasses or a hat to protect from the sun.
   - **Poncho or Umbrella**: Tokyo Disney Resort experiences occasional rain, especially during the summer months. A lightweight poncho or small umbrella can come in handy, especially since the

park rarely cancels rides or shows for rain.

2. **What to Leave Behind:**
   - **Large Bags**: You'll want to keep your bag light. Leave large bags behind and opt for a small backpack or crossbody bag. This will make it easier to move through crowds and ride attractions comfortably.
   - **Expensive Jewelry**: While Disney parks are safe, you don't want to risk losing valuable jewelry or accessories. Leave them at home to avoid worrying about them during the day.

Weather-Appropriate Packing Tips

1. **Summer (June to August):**
   - **What to Bring**: Light clothing, breathable fabrics, sunscreen, hat, sunglasses, and comfortable sandals. The summer heat can be intense, so make sure you're prepared for high temperatures and humidity.
   - **What to Avoid**: Heavy clothing that can make you overheat. It's also wise to avoid bringing anything that might get ruined in the rain, as summer showers are common.

2. **Winter (December to February)**:
   - **What to Bring**: Warm clothing, jackets, scarves, and gloves. The temperature can drop significantly in the winter months, especially in the evenings.
   - **What to Avoid**: Heavy boots or anything too bulky that could make walking uncomfortable.

3. **Rainy Season (May to June)**:
   - **What to Bring**: Light rain jacket or poncho, waterproof shoes, and an umbrella. The rainy season can be unpredictable, but it doesn't mean you can't enjoy the park—just be prepared to stay dry!
   - **What to Avoid**: Items that are easily damaged by rain, like expensive electronics without waterproof protection.

Language and Cultural Tips

Although many Cast Members at Tokyo Disney Resort speak English, knowing a few basic Japanese phrases and understanding some local customs can go a long way in making your experience even more magical. Here are some tips to help you navigate the resort and communicate with ease.

Basic Japanese Phrases to Know

While you don't need to be fluent in Japanese, learning a few common phrases can help you feel more confident and connected with the local culture. Here are some basic phrases that will come in handy:

1. **Hello / Goodbye**
    - こんにちは **(Konnichiwa)**: Hello
    - さようなら **(Sayōnara)**: Goodbye
    - お疲れ様でした **(Otsukaresama deshita)**: A polite way to say "Thank you for your hard work" (useful for thanking staff).

2. **Thank You**
    - ありがとう **(Arigatou)**: Thank you
    - ありがとうございます **(Arigatou gozaimasu)**: A more polite way of saying "thank you" (use this in most situations).

3. **Excuse Me / Sorry**
    - すみません **(Sumimasen)**: Excuse me, or I'm sorry (a very versatile phrase for getting attention or apologizing).

4. **Please**
    - お願いします **(Onegaishimasu)**: Please (use when making a request, e.g., "Please give me a ticket").

5. **Yes / No**
    - **はい (Hai)**: Yes
    - **いいえ (Iie)**: No
6. **How Much is This?**
    - **これいくらですか (Kore ikura desu ka?)**: How much is this? (Use this when asking about prices).
7. **Where is…?**
    - **…はどこですか (… wa doko desu ka?)**: Where is…? (Great for asking for directions, such as "Where is Space Mountain?").

Knowing these key phrases will not only help you navigate the resort but also show respect for the local culture. The Japanese appreciate when visitors make an effort to speak their language, even if it's just a few words.

Understanding Japanese Customs and Etiquette

1. **Politeness is Key**
    - Japanese culture places a strong emphasis on respect and politeness. Always try to be courteous, especially when interacting with Cast Members or fellow visitors. A little bow, a smile, and a polite "arigatou" go a long way.

2. **Queueing**
   - Japan is famous for its **orderly queues**. At Tokyo Disney Resort, you'll notice that everyone waits their turn in line with no pushing or cutting. When you're in line for rides or shows, make sure to follow the line without crowding others. It's considered respectful to maintain space.

3. **Taking Photos**
   - While it's okay to take photos throughout the parks, be mindful of where you take them. Some attractions and areas (like **dark rides** or **character meet-and-greets**) may have restrictions, so make sure to follow the guidelines.
   - Avoid using flash photography in dark indoor areas to prevent disturbing other guests.

4. **Tipping is Uncommon**
   - Unlike in some other countries, **tipping** is not a practice in Japan. Instead, the culture values excellent service, and staff at Tokyo Disney Resort are very attentive. You don't need to worry about tipping—just show appreciation by saying "thank you" in Japanese or simply with a smile.

5. **Food Etiquette**
    - In Japan, it's common to eat quietly and respectfully. At Tokyo Disney Resort, you'll notice that food courts and restaurants are generally clean and well-maintained, so try to keep your eating area tidy as a courtesy. It's also customary to finish all your food, especially rice, to show respect for the meal.
    - **Eating while walking**: While eating on the go is common in some places, it's best to sit down in designated eating areas when enjoying your food at the resort, as walking around while eating might be considered impolite.

Tech Tips

The **Tokyo Disney Resort app** and other tech tools can make your visit even more enjoyable and convenient. From skipping the lines to making mobile payments, here are some **tech tips** to enhance your experience and make your time at the resort stress-free.

Best Apps for Tokyo Disney Resort

1. **Tokyo Disney Resort App**
    - **What it Does**: This app is a must-have! It provides real-time information about ride wait times, show schedules,

restaurant menus, mobile food ordering, and much more. You can even use the app for interactive maps to help you navigate the park.

- **How to Use It**: Download the app before your trip (it's free for both iOS and Android). Make sure to enable notifications to get the latest updates on wait times, closures, and special offers.

2. **Disney FastPass**
    - **What it Does**: The **FastPass** system allows you to skip the regular lines for certain rides by reserving a time slot in advance. While you can no longer use paper FastPasses, the digital FastPass system through the Tokyo Disney Resort App allows you to reserve spots for popular attractions like **Big Thunder Mountain** and **Space Mountain**.
    - **How to Use It**: Once you're in the park, open the app and select available FastPasses for your favorite rides. Be aware that there's a limited number of FastPasses, so plan ahead and book as soon as you're eligible.

3. **Tokyo Disney Resort's Mobile Food Ordering**
    - **What it Does**: This feature in the app allows you to order food at select restaurants in advance, skipping the lines at counter-service spots. It's especially

useful during lunch hours when the food courts and restaurants tend to get crowded.

- **How to Use It**: Select your meal from the menu in the app, choose a pick-up time, and head straight to the designated pick-up counter when your food is ready. This saves time and lets you enjoy more attractions!

4. **Google Maps and Translation Apps**

    - **What it Does**: While the Tokyo Disney Resort App is excellent for in-park info, you may want to use **Google Maps** for directions to and from the resort or to explore Tokyo after your visit. If you're unsure about something, **Google Translate** or similar apps can help with language barriers.

    - **How to Use It**: Google Maps will give you accurate walking directions within the resort, and translation apps allow you to instantly translate Japanese to English. This is especially helpful when you're reading signs or trying to order food at a Japanese restaurant.

Using Mobile Payments and Other Tech Solutions for Convenience

1. **Mobile Payments (Suica, Pasmo, and Apple Pay)**
   - **What it Does**: Tokyo Disney Resort has implemented **mobile payment systems** that make it easier for visitors to pay for goods and services without carrying cash. Suica and Pasmo are contactless cards that work like digital wallets, and **Apple Pay** is widely accepted in the resort.
   - **How to Use It**: Download the **Suica** or **Pasmo** apps or link your **Apple Pay** to your phone for easy payments at shops, food stalls, and even some ride queues. It's a quick and efficient way to manage your spending without worrying about cash.

2. **Contactless Payments at Restaurants and Shops**
   - **What it Does**: Most shops and restaurants at Tokyo Disney Resort accept **contactless payment** methods, including Suica, Pasmo, and Apple Pay. This is incredibly convenient, especially when you're looking to buy merchandise or grab a quick snack.

- **How to Use It**: Simply tap your phone or card on the payment terminal for a quick, seamless transaction.

3. **Wi-Fi Access**

    - **What it Does**: Tokyo Disney Resort offers **free Wi-Fi** in many areas of the park, including at restaurants and main attractions. Staying connected helps you stay updated with ride wait times and helps with using the app for FastPass and food ordering.

    - **How to Use It**: Connect to the **Tokyo Disney Resort Wi-Fi** in the park. You may need to log in through the app or a web page on your phone when you first connect.

Seasonal Events and Parades

There's no better time to experience the magic of **Tokyo Disney Resort** than during its seasonal celebrations. The resort transforms with spectacular decorations, special events, parades, and unforgettable shows. Whether it's the festive cheer of **Christmas**, the thrill of **Halloween**, or the excitement of **New Year's**, every season offers something extraordinary. In this section, I'll take you through all the festive fun, must-see parades, and exclusive events in 2025 that will make your visit extra magical!

Holiday Celebrations

Tokyo Disney Resort knows how to throw a party, especially during the holidays! The park is filled with festive decorations, exclusive shows, and themed events that will make you feel like you're stepping into a winter wonderland or a spooky, fun-filled Halloween night. Let's dive into the **special events during Christmas, New Year's, and Halloween.**

Special Events During Christmas, New Year's, and Halloween

1. **Christmas Celebrations (November to December)**
   - **Why It's Special**: Christmas at Tokyo Disney Resort is a magical, festive celebration filled with gorgeous decorations, holiday treats, and special shows. The entire resort becomes a winter wonderland, with sparkling lights, themed music, and the joyous spirit of the season.
   - **What to Expect**:
     - **Holiday Decor**: **Cinderella Castle** is decked out in twinkling lights and snowflakes, while **DisneySea's Mediterranean Harbor** is adorned with Christmas trees and festive banners.
     - **Exclusive Shows**: Don't miss the **"Disney's Christmas Stories" Parade** and the **"A Christmas Fantasy" show**, where beloved Disney characters take center stage in a beautiful winter-themed celebration.
     - **Character Meet-and-Greets**: Santa Mickey, Minnie, and other Disney characters make special appearances in their Christmas attire, giving guests a chance for festive photos.

- **Holiday Treats and Merchandise**: Indulge in **seasonal treats** like Mickey-shaped **gingerbread cookies, hot chocolate**, and **holiday-themed snacks**. Be sure to grab **exclusive Christmas merchandise**—from plush toys to limited-edition holiday mugs.

2. **New Year's Celebrations (December 31 to January 1)**

    - **Why It's Special**: Tokyo Disney Resort ushers in the New Year with vibrant festivities and special performances that blend Japanese tradition with Disney magic. It's a time for new beginnings, and the celebrations are as grand as you'd expect.

    - **What to Expect**:

- **New Year's Day Countdown**: Celebrate the transition into the New Year with **special fireworks** and a **countdown party** in the park. At midnight, watch as fireworks light up the sky over **Cinderella Castle** in Tokyo Disneyland.

- **Traditional Japanese Elements**: Experience Japanese New Year traditions, including special **shrine offerings** and themed decorations at **Tokyo DisneySea**.

- **Exclusive Character Appearances**: Meet Mickey and friends dressed in their **New Year's outfits**, often featuring traditional Japanese attire like **kimonos**.

- **Limited-Time Merchandise**: Pick up **exclusive New Year-themed items** like **year-of-the-animal merchandise** and **lucky charms**.

3. **Halloween Celebrations (September to October)**

    - **Why It's Special**: Tokyo Disney Resort goes all out for Halloween, creating a spooky and fun atmosphere with themed decorations, character costumes, and unique experiences that transport you to a world of enchantment and excitement.

    - **What to Expect**:

- **Spooky Decor**: The park is transformed into a Halloween wonderland with giant pumpkins, eerie lights, and spooky music that fills the air.

- **Halloween Parades and Shows**: Don't miss the **"Disney Halloween" Parade** featuring villains, ghosts, and spooky Disney characters. The **Haunted Mansion Holiday** is also a must-see, blending **Jack Skellington** and his crew with the classic haunted house experience.

- **Exclusive Character Meet-and-Greets**: During Halloween, Disney characters wear their most creative costumes. Get your photo taken with **Mickey as a pumpkin**, **Minnie as a witch**, and **Goofy as a ghost**.

- **Halloween-Themed Food**: Treat yourself to spooky snacks like **Halloween-themed popcorn** and **spooky cakes**.

Must-See Parades, Shows, and Fireworks

Parades, shows, and fireworks are the heartbeat of the magic at Tokyo Disney Resort, especially during the holiday seasons. These events bring joy, laughter, and excitement to all visitors, creating moments of wonder and awe. Here's how to catch the most magical performances during your visit.

Best Times to Catch Parades and Fireworks

1. **Arrive Early for Parades**
   - Parades at Tokyo Disney Resort are extremely popular, so make sure to arrive at the parade route at least **30 minutes to an hour before showtime** to get a great spot. If you want a front-row view, aim for spots near **Main Street** (Tokyo Disneyland) or **Mediterranean Harbor** (Tokyo DisneySea).
   - **Parade Showtimes**: The parades typically run at set times throughout the day, and their schedule can vary, especially during peak seasons like Christmas and Halloween. Always

check the Tokyo Disney Resort app for the most up-to-date information on showtimes.

2. **Fireworks at Night**
    - Tokyo Disney Resort offers **amazing fireworks shows** throughout the year, with some of the best being during the **New Year's** and **Christmas celebrations**. Fireworks are typically launched from the **Mediterranean Harbor** (DisneySea) or around **Cinderella Castle** (Disneyland).
    - **Best Viewing Spots**: For a clear view of the fireworks, head to **Cinderella Castle** in Tokyo Disneyland or **Mediterranean Harbor** in DisneySea. If you want a more peaceful experience, consider watching from the **American Waterfront** in DisneySea, where you can avoid the heavy crowds.

Where to Sit for the Best Views

1. **For Parades**:
    - **Tokyo Disneyland**: The best spots for viewing parades are along the **World Bazaar** area or near the **Hub Plaza** in front of **Cinderella Castle**. These areas offer a central view of the parade floats, and you'll be able to enjoy the full spectacle.
    - **Tokyo DisneySea**: **Mediterranean Harbor** provides an excellent viewing area for parades. Make sure to arrive early for the best spots near

the water, where you'll get a perfect view of the floats, characters, and performers.

2. **For Fireworks**:

    - **Tokyo Disneyland**: The **Hub Plaza** in front of **Cinderella Castle** is a great spot for watching the fireworks. If you want to avoid the crowds, try viewing them from **Tomorrowland** or **Fantasyland**—you won't miss the show, and you'll have a bit more space.

    - **Tokyo DisneySea**: The **Mediterranean Harbor** is where most fireworks are launched, so being near the water gives you the best experience. For a quieter experience, head toward **American Waterfront**, where you can still enjoy the fireworks without the massive crowds.

Themed Events and Festivals in 2025

2025 is shaping up to be a year full of exciting, exclusive events that you won't want to miss. Here are the **special 2025-only events** that will add extra magic to your visit.

Special 2025-Only Events You Shouldn't Miss

1. **Tokyo Disney Resort's 40th Anniversary Celebration**

- **What It Is**: 2025 marks the **40th anniversary** of Tokyo Disney Resort, and it's going to be a year-long celebration filled with **exclusive parades**, **special shows**, and **limited-edition merchandise**.
- **What to Expect**:
  - **Anniversary-Themed Parades**: Look forward to a **new parade** that will showcase beloved characters in fresh, anniversary-inspired costumes. Expect dazzling floats, special effects, and a celebration of the resort's rich history.
  - **Special Shows and Performances**: The "Tokyo Disney Resort 40th Anniversary Show" will highlight the magical journey of the resort, featuring live performances, fireworks, and projections on iconic landmarks like **Cinderella Castle**.
  - **Limited-Edition Merchandise**: The 40th anniversary will bring **exclusive anniversary pins**, plush toys, and apparel that commemorate the milestone.

2. **Disney's 100th Anniversary Celebrations (2025)**
   - **What It Is**: 2025 will also mark **100 years of Disney magic**, and Tokyo Disney Resort will join in the global celebration with **exclusive events**, including special parades and themed attractions.

- **What to Expect:**
- **Centennial-Themed Parades**: Expect a grand parade featuring **classic Disney characters** and iconic moments from Disney's history.

- **Special Edition Merchandise**: Celebrate Disney's century-long legacy with exclusive **100th anniversary merchandise**, including collectible items like commemorative mugs, plushies, and limited-edition artwork.

- **Once-in-a-Lifetime Shows**: Experience a **centennial show** that will feature music, storytelling, and fireworks that span the history of Disney films and characters.

3. **Spring and Summer Festivals**
   - **Spring at Tokyo Disneyland**: The **spring season** in 2025 will include the vibrant **Flower and Garden Festival**, where beautiful flowers will bloom across the parks. Special performances and themed dining experiences will celebrate the season of renewal.

   - **Summer at Tokyo DisneySea**: Summer in 2025 will bring a **Water Parade**, featuring aquatic-themed floats and live performances that celebrate the fun of summer. You'll be treated to **cool treats**, and there will be seasonal food items designed to keep you refreshed during the hot months.

Beyond the Parks

While Tokyo Disney Resort is undeniably magical, the excitement of Tokyo doesn't stop there. Beyond the resort, the city pulses with vibrant culture, rich history, and unforgettable experiences waiting to be explored. Whether you want to delve into Japan's fascinating history, shop in bustling districts, or embark on day trips to iconic locations, there's something for every type of traveler.

Let's take a deeper dive into the **must-see attractions** and the cultural experiences that will make your trip to Tokyo even more extraordinary.

Exploring Tokyo Beyond Disney

Tokyo is a city of contrasts: modern skyscrapers stand side by side with centuries-old temples and shrines, bustling shopping districts meet tranquil gardens, and cutting-edge technology mixes with traditional culture. Here are some essential recommendations for exploring this dynamic city beyond the gates of Disney.

Must-See Attractions in Tokyo: Shrines, Museums, and Shopping

1. **Meiji Shrine (Meiji Jingu)**
   - **Why Visit**: Nestled in the heart of Tokyo's bustling **Shibuya** district, **Meiji Shrine** is one of Japan's most important Shinto shrines. Dedicated to Emperor Meiji and Empress Shoken, this peaceful oasis offers a serene escape from the city's fast pace.
   - **What to Do**:
     - Stroll through the **torii gates** that mark the entrance to the shrine.
     - Explore the **sprawling grounds** surrounded by lush forests, home to over 100,000 trees.
     - Participate in traditional rituals, like **writing wishes** on wooden plaques (ema) and hanging them at the shrine.
   - **Pro Tip**: Visit early in the morning or late in the afternoon to avoid crowds and experience a more peaceful atmosphere.

2. **Senso-ji Temple (Asakusa)**
   - **Why Visit**: Located in the **Asakusa** district, **Senso-ji** is Tokyo's oldest temple and one of the most famous

landmarks in the city. Established in the 7th century, it is dedicated to **Kannon**, the Goddess of Mercy.

- **What to Do**:
    - Wander down **Nakamise Street**, lined with traditional shops selling souvenirs, snacks, and crafts.
    - Explore the temple's grand **Kaminarimon gate**, which is a striking symbol of the temple.
    - Light an **incense stick** for good luck and try your hand at **omikuji** (fortune-telling).
- **Pro Tip**: Take time to explore the nearby **Asakusa Culture and Tourist Information Center**, where you can learn more about the area's rich history.

3. **The National Museum of Tokyo (Ueno)**
    - **Why Visit**: If you're keen on experiencing Japan's culture and history, the **National Museum of Tokyo** in **Ueno Park** is a must-visit. This renowned museum houses over 110,000 artifacts, showcasing Japan's ancient art and cultural heritage.
    - **What to Do**:
        - Marvel at priceless collections of **samurai armor, ancient**

pottery, and **Buddhist sculptures**.
  - Check out **special exhibits**, which often feature works from global artists.
  - After the museum, wander around **Ueno Park** to enjoy the scenic landscapes and the beautiful **Shinobazu Pond**.
- **Pro Tip**: Ueno Park is a great place to visit during **cherry blossom season** (March-April), where the park becomes a sea of pink blossoms.

4. **Shibuya and Harajuku Districts**
   - **Why Visit**: For a more contemporary taste of Tokyo, head to the **Shibuya** and **Harajuku** districts, which are brimming with youthful energy, street fashion, and vibrant city life.
   - **What to Do**:
     - **Shibuya Crossing**: Cross the world-famous **Shibuya Crossing**, one of the busiest pedestrian intersections in the world.
     - **Shopping**: Explore the trendy boutiques and shops of **Harajuku**, which is famous for its unique and quirky fashion.

- **Meiji Shrine**: After shopping, head to the nearby **Meiji Shrine** for a peaceful contrast to the bustling districts.

- **Pro Tip**: Visit **Takeshita Street** in Harajuku for some of the best street food, quirky fashion, and fun accessories.

5. **Odaiba: Tokyo's Futuristic Island**

    - **Why Visit**: Located in Tokyo Bay, **Odaiba** is a man-made island known for its futuristic architecture, shopping malls, entertainment complexes, and great views of the **Rainbow Bridge** and **Tokyo Bay**.

    - **What to Do**:

        - Visit the **teamLab Borderless Museum**, an immersive digital art experience that is visually stunning and completely unique.

        - Relax at **Odaiba Seaside Park** and take in the views of the bay.

        - Check out **Gundam Base Tokyo**, where you can see a life-sized **Gundam statue** and shop for **Gundam-related merchandise**.

        - **Pro Tip**: The **Palette Town Ferris Wheel** offers breathtaking views of

Tokyo from above—perfect for an evening ride.

Top Cultural Experiences in the City

Tokyo is a cultural hub, blending ancient traditions with cutting-edge modernity. Here are some cultural experiences you won't want to miss.

1. **Sumo Wrestling**

    - **Why Experience It**: Sumo is Japan's national sport, and experiencing a live match is a unique way to connect with Japanese culture.

    - **Where to Go**: The **Ryogoku Kokugikan** stadium in **Sumo Town** is where the major tournaments take place, typically in **January, May, and September**.

    - **What to Do**:

        - Watch a sumo match and witness the intensity of this ancient sport.

        - Visit **Sumo museums** in Ryogoku, like the **Sumo Museum**, which displays the history of sumo.

    - **Pro Tip**: If you're visiting during the off-season, head to a sumo training stable (called **beya**) for a unique behind-the-scenes experience. Some stables offer public viewings.

2. **Japanese Tea Ceremony**
    - **Why Experience It**: The **Japanese tea ceremony** is a centuries-old tradition that emphasizes mindfulness, etiquette, and the beauty of nature. Participating in a tea ceremony offers a peaceful, introspective experience.
    - **Where to Go**: There are several places in Tokyo that offer traditional tea ceremonies, including **Happo-en Garden** and **The Imperial Hotel**.
    - **What to Do**:
        - Learn about the preparation of **matcha** tea.
        - Experience the rituals, from the movements of the tea master to the beauty of the utensils.
    - **Pro Tip**: Many tea ceremonies include a **kaiseki meal**, a multi-course meal that complements the tea, so be sure to come hungry!

3. **Kabuki Theater**
    - **Why Experience It**: Kabuki is one of Japan's oldest performing arts, combining music, dance, and drama to tell stories from Japanese folklore and history.

- **Where to Go**: The **Kabuki-za Theatre** in **Ginza** is Tokyo's premier venue for Kabuki performances.
- **What to Do**:
  - Watch a **Kabuki play**, which often involves intricate costumes, dramatic performances, and live music.
  - Take a short **Kabuki workshop** if you're interested in learning about the art form.
- **Pro Tip**: While the full Kabuki performances can be lengthy, you can purchase tickets for just part of the show (known as the **"morning show"**), which is more affordable and less time-consuming.

Day Trips from Tokyo Disney Resort

Tokyo is not only a city of wonder; it's also a perfect starting point for exploring Japan's iconic locations. Whether you're looking for natural beauty, historic landmarks, or a tranquil escape, these **day trips from Tokyo Disney Resort** will enhance your adventure and offer a deeper dive into the richness of Japan.

Visiting Mount Fuji

1. **Why Visit Mount Fuji**

   - Mount Fuji is Japan's tallest and most iconic mountain, revered for its beauty and spiritual significance. It's an ideal day trip for nature lovers and those seeking to connect with Japan's countryside.

2. **How to Get There**

   - **Travel Time**: It takes about **2 to 2.5 hours** to reach **Mount Fuji** from Tokyo Disney Resort by train or bus.

   - **Pro Tip**: Take the **Fuji Excursion Limited Express** from **Shinjuku Station**, which will take you directly to the **Fujisan Station** for a closer view of the mountain.

3. **What to Do**

   - **Climb Mount Fuji**: If you're visiting during the climbing season (July to early September), you can trek to the summit for stunning panoramic views.

   - **Explore the Fuji Five Lakes Area**: The **Fuji Five Lakes** region offers beautiful lake views of Mount Fuji, as well as hiking trails, hot springs, and quaint villages.

- **Visit Chureito Pagoda**: One of the most picturesque spots to take a photo of Mount Fuji, with the **pagoda** in the foreground and the mountain rising behind it.

Kyoto: The Cultural Capital of Japan

1. **Why Visit Kyoto**
   - Kyoto is known for its ancient temples, traditional tea houses, and tranquil atmosphere. It's a place where you can step back in time and experience the cultural heart of Japan.

2. **How to Get There**
   - **Travel Time**: It takes about **2.5 to 3 hours** to reach Kyoto from Tokyo Disney Resort by **shinkansen** (bullet train).
   - **Pro Tip**: Kyoto is best explored at a leisurely pace, so if you have a full day, you can explore key spots like the **Golden Pavilion**, **Fushimi Inari Shrine**, and **Arashiyama Bamboo Grove**.

3. **What to Do**
   - **Visit Kinkaku-ji** (Golden Pavilion): The serene and beautiful **Golden Pavilion** is one of Kyoto's most iconic landmarks.

- **Walk through Fushimi Inari Shrine**: Walk the mesmerizing paths lined with **thousands of red torii gates** at Fushimi Inari, one of Kyoto's most famous shrines.

- **Explore the Arashiyama Bamboo Grove**: Take a stroll through the **bamboo forests** and experience the peaceful atmosphere.

Other Iconic Locations in Japan

1. **Nara**: Famous for its **free-roaming deer**, **Todai-ji Temple**, and **Nara Park**. It's just about **45 minutes** from Kyoto by train.

2. **Hakone**: Known for its **hot springs** and breathtaking views of Mount Fuji, **Hakone** is the perfect spot to unwind in nature. It's about **90 minutes** from Tokyo Disney Resort.

Safety and Accessibility

Visiting Tokyo Disney Resort is an exciting and magical experience for everyone, and ensuring that your trip is safe and comfortable is our top priority. Whether you're visiting with young children, have accessibility needs, or are navigating health guidelines, this section will guide you through everything you need to know to ensure a smooth and enjoyable visit. From health and safety updates to services for guests with disabilities, we'll cover all the essential information to help you feel well-prepared and at ease.

Health and Safety Guidelines

Your safety is paramount, and Tokyo Disney Resort has introduced several measures to protect guests in 2025. These guidelines ensure that you can focus on enjoying your time at the resort while keeping your health and well-being in mind. Let's go over the most important health and safety measures currently in place.

COVID-19 Updates and Travel Precautions

1. **Current Health and Safety Protocols (2025)**
2. Tokyo Disney Resort follows the latest public health guidance to protect guests, including hygiene protocols, social distancing, and vaccination requirements where applicable. As

the situation evolves, updates to these measures are made to ensure the safety of all visitors.

3. **Face Masks and Social Distancing**

    - **What to Expect**: While masks are not always required outdoors, they may be required in certain indoor spaces or crowded areas, especially for health-sensitive guests. You'll find clearly marked areas where masks should be worn.

    - **Social Distancing**: Physical distancing measures will still be observed in many parts of the resort, including queue lines, seating areas, and restaurants. In some places, you may see markers on the ground to help maintain safe spacing.

    - **Health Screenings**: Expect health screenings at entry points to the parks and other venues. You may be asked to complete a brief **health questionnaire** before entering.

4. **Enhanced Cleaning and Sanitization**

    - **Frequent Cleaning**: Tokyo Disney Resort has implemented enhanced cleaning procedures across the parks, including disinfecting high-touch surfaces, restrooms, and ride vehicles regularly throughout the day.

    - **Hand Sanitizer Stations**: You'll find **hand sanitizer stations** conveniently located around the park, especially near ride entrances, dining areas, and high-traffic spots.

5. **Vaccination and Testing**
    - **Vaccination**: While vaccination is not mandatory, visitors are encouraged to stay informed about any travel restrictions or requirements regarding vaccinations, especially for international guests.
    - **Testing**: Guests may be asked to provide proof of a negative COVID-19 test prior to entry, depending on travel guidelines. Stay updated through the resort's official website or the Tokyo Disney Resort app.

Other Health and Safety Tips

1. **Stay Hydrated**
2. Tokyo Disney Resort can get quite warm, especially in summer. Be sure to drink plenty of water throughout the day, especially if you're spending a lot of time outside. Bottled water is available throughout the park, and there are refill stations for water bottles to help keep you hydrated.
3. **Sun Protection**
4. The sun can be strong, particularly during the summer months. Apply sunscreen regularly and wear a hat or sunglasses to protect yourself from

UV rays. Be mindful of **sunstroke**—take breaks in the shade and rest as needed.

5. **Personal First-Aid Kits**
6. It's always a good idea to carry a small **personal first-aid kit** with essentials like band-aids, pain relievers, and any prescription medications. While the resort has medical facilities, having these items on hand can be useful for minor issues.
7. **Emergency Medical Services**
8. Tokyo Disney Resort has **on-site medical services**. If you need medical attention, you can visit one of the First-Aid stations or contact a Cast Member for assistance. **Emergency response teams** are available throughout the park for urgent medical needs.

Accessible Travel Tips

Tokyo Disney Resort strives to make the park accessible for all guests. From mobility assistance to services for guests with disabilities, the resort offers a variety of resources to ensure that everyone has an enjoyable and comfortable experience.

Services for Guests with Disabilities

1. **Disability Access Service (DAS)**
    - **What It Is**: The **Disability Access Service (DAS)** is a program that allows guests with disabilities to schedule ride

times and reduce wait times for attractions. Instead of standing in a long queue, guests can receive a return time for their desired attractions.

- **How to Use It**:
    - Visit the **Guest Relations** office at the park's entrance to request DAS.
    - A Cast Member will assist you in selecting the attractions you want to visit and will provide you with a return time for each.
- **Note**: DAS is available for guests who have a disability that prevents them from waiting in a standard queue. If you're unsure whether you qualify, Cast Members are available to answer any questions.

2. **Accessible Restrooms**
    - **Where to Find Them**: The resort has **accessible restrooms** throughout both Tokyo Disneyland and Tokyo DisneySea. These facilities are designed for ease of use and ensure a comfortable experience for guests with mobility challenges.
    - **Pro Tip**: Check the **Tokyo Disney Resort app** for restroom locations or ask a Cast Member for directions.

3. **Wheelchair and ECV Rentals**

    - **Wheelchair Rentals**: Tokyo Disney Resort offers **complimentary wheelchairs** for guests who need them. These can be obtained at the **Guest Relations** office at the park entrance.

    - **Electric Conveyance Vehicles (ECVs)**: If you require an **ECV**, you can rent one from the park. Be sure to arrive early as there is limited availability.

    - **Pro Tip**: ECVs can be reserved in advance through the official Tokyo Disney Resort website to ensure availability on the day of your visit.

4. **Service Animal Policies**

    - **What to Expect**: Guests who use service animals are welcome to bring their animals to the resort. Service animals are allowed in most areas of the park, including attractions, dining areas, and shows.

    - **Important Guidelines**:

        - Service animals must remain on a leash or harness at all times.

        - Cast Members will assist with navigating areas that may be more challenging, such as specific attractions or dining areas.

160 |TOKYO DISNEY RESORT

- **Pro Tip**: If you need any special accommodations, it's always helpful to inform a Cast Member in advance.

Mobility Assistance and Special Needs Information

1. **Parking for Guests with Disabilities**
   - **Accessible Parking Spaces**: The resort offers **designated accessible parking** spaces for guests with disabilities. These are located close to the entrances of both Tokyo Disneyland and Tokyo DisneySea.
   - **How to Access**: Accessible parking spaces are available on a first-come, first-served basis. If you're using public transportation, be sure to ask for information about accessible options at your hotel or the resort's transit station.

2. **Accessible Attractions**
   - Tokyo Disney Resort is equipped with many **accessible attractions**. This includes rides that are designed for easy access for wheelchair users, and there are even special vehicles for certain attractions to ensure comfort.
   - **Notable Attractions with Accessible Options**:

- **Pirates of the Caribbean** (both parks)
- **It's a Small World** (both parks)
- **The Many Adventures of Winnie the Pooh** (Tokyo Disneyland)
- **Pro Tip**: For more detailed information on specific ride accessibility, visit the **Guest Relations** or check the **Tokyo Disney Resort app** for up-to-date info.

3. **Quiet Spaces**
    - Tokyo Disney Resort also offers **quiet spaces** for guests who need a peaceful break from the crowds. These areas are designed for those who may experience sensory overload or need a rest in a calm environment.
    - **Where to Find Them**: Quiet spaces are available throughout the resort. You can ask any Cast Member to direct you to the nearest area.

Childcare and Family Services

Tokyo Disney Resort is a family-friendly destination, and they have a variety of services designed to make your visit more convenient and enjoyable, especially if you're visiting with young children. From baby care stations to family services, the resort has you covered.

Baby Care Stations and Family-Friendly Services

1. **Baby Care Centers**
   - **What's Available**: Tokyo Disney Resort provides **Baby Care Centers** in both Tokyo Disneyland and Tokyo DisneySea. These centers are equipped with changing tables, nursing rooms, and comfortable seating for parents.
   - **What to Expect**:
     - Private **nursing rooms** with seating for mothers to breastfeed in a calm and comfortable space.
     - **Changing stations** with baby essentials available for your convenience.
     - **Microwave** and **hot water** stations for heating up baby food and formula.
   - **Pro Tip**: Baby care centers are located near major attractions, and you can find their exact locations in the **Tokyo Disney Resort app** or by asking a Cast Member.

2. **Stroller Rentals**
   - **What's Available**: The resort offers **stroller rentals** for families visiting

with young children. Strollers are available for rent at the **Guest Relations** areas in both parks.

- **Pro Tip**: If you don't want to carry a stroller with you, consider renting one for the day. Keep in mind that **stroller sizes are standardized**, so be sure to check the rental policy for any restrictions on the type of stroller.

3. **Family Services**

    - **Child Swap**: For families with younger children who may not meet the height requirement for certain rides, **Child Swap** allows one parent to wait with the child while the other enjoys the ride. When the first parent returns, they can switch without having to wait in line again.

    - **Family Rest Areas**: There are designated **family rest areas** throughout both parks, where you can relax and take a break from the excitement. These areas are perfect for resting with young children or grandparents.

Conclusion

Your upcoming trip to **Tokyo Disney Resort** is sure to be a magical adventure, filled with unforgettable memories and joy. As you prepare for your visit, I want to leave you with a sense of excitement and confidence. In this section, I'll recap the must-dos, share personal insights, and provide expert advice to ensure that your experience is as seamless and enjoyable as possible. Let's take one last look at the important tips and final words of inspiration to help you embrace the magic of Tokyo Disney Resort!

Making the Most of Your Magical Trip

Tokyo Disney Resort is a place where magic comes to life, and you'll want to make every moment count. Whether you're traveling with family, friends, or as a solo adventurer, there's something for everyone. To make sure you're ready to get the most out of your visit, here's a **recap of the must-dos** to keep in mind.

1. **Start Early and Plan Ahead**
    - **Why It's Important**: The early bird truly catches the magic at Tokyo Disney Resort! Arriving early will help you beat the crowds and get a jump on your favorite attractions. This will also give you a chance to take advantage of lower

wait times and maximize your time in the parks.

- **What to Do**: Be at the gates before the parks open to experience **popular attractions** such as **Space Mountain**, **Big Thunder Mountain**, and **Pirates of the Caribbean** without long waits. Use your first few hours to enjoy these top rides before the crowds arrive.

2. **Use the Tokyo Disney Resort App**

    - **Why It's Important**: The **Tokyo Disney Resort app** is an invaluable tool for navigating the parks. It's essential for checking **ride wait times**, **show schedules**, and **mobile food ordering**. Download it before you arrive and familiarize yourself with the features to make your visit as smooth as possible.

    - **What to Do**:
        - Monitor **real-time updates** on ride wait times.
        - **Reserve dining** using mobile ordering and FastPass for rides.
        - Check the **interactive map** to navigate the parks and find the nearest restrooms, food stations, and attractions.

3. **Don't Miss the Parades and Shows**
    - **Why It's Important**: The parades and shows at Tokyo Disney Resort are **iconic** and **not to be missed**. These performances bring the magic of Disney to life in ways that are truly breathtaking.
    - **What to Do**: Plan ahead for the **Disney parades**, especially during the evening when the magic is amplified with **lights** and **fireworks**. Find a great spot along the parade route or near **Cinderella Castle** to catch the action.
    - **Pro Tip**: Arrive early for the best views, and keep an eye on the Tokyo Disney Resort app for the latest schedule updates.

4. **Take Time for Relaxation**
    - **Why It's Important**: While Tokyo Disney Resort is full of excitement, it's just as important to take breaks and enjoy the peaceful corners of the parks. Don't rush from one attraction to the next—take moments to soak in the ambiance.
    - **What to Do**: Head to areas like **Tokyo DisneySea's Mediterranean Harbor** or **Fantasyland** in Tokyo Disneyland for a relaxing stroll. Find a quiet bench or café to enjoy a snack or simply people-watch. It's these small moments of relaxation that will help

balance out your adventure and give you the energy to keep exploring.

5. **Capture the Magic**

- **Why It's Important**: One of the most exciting parts of visiting Tokyo Disney Resort is collecting memories. Whether it's photos with your favorite characters or shots of the **iconic landmarks**, make sure to capture the magic.

- **What to Do**:
    - Take photos in front of **Cinderella Castle**, **Pirates of the Caribbean**, and other must-see locations.
    - Consider using **Disney PhotoPass** to capture professional-quality photos throughout the park.
    - Don't forget to snap some candid photos during the parades and shows to relive the magic when you return home.

Having visited Tokyo Disney Resort myself, I want to share a few **personal insights and insider tips** that will make your experience even better. These tips will help you navigate the parks like a pro and ensure you're making the most of your time at the resort.

1. **Prioritize FastPasses for High-Demand Rides**
    - **Why It's Important**: FastPass is a game-changer, especially for the most popular attractions. If you plan to visit Tokyo Disneyland or DisneySea during peak times, securing a FastPass will help you avoid long waits and ensure you get the most out of your day.
    - **What to Do**:
        - Head to the FastPass distribution points for rides like **Space Mountain**, **Indiana Jones Adventure**, and **Splash Mountain** early to secure your spots.
        - Once you've used a FastPass, immediately grab another for a different attraction, keeping your day organized and efficient.
2. **Take Advantage of Single Rider Lines**
    - **Why It's Important**: Single Rider lines are a **great option** if you're traveling solo or if you don't mind riding separately from your group. These lines are often much shorter and help you save time.
    - **What to Do**: Look for Single Rider options at **Big Thunder Mountain**, **Splash Mountain**, and **Indiana**

Jones Adventure, where they are offered. You'll often be able to hop onto the ride much faster.

3. **Bring Snacks and Water**
   - **Why It's Important**: Disney food is fantastic, but sometimes waiting in line for meals can take up valuable time. By packing snacks and water, you can keep your energy levels high without missing out on the fun.
   - **What to Do**:
     - Bring some **granola bars**, **fruit snacks**, or **trail mix** to keep you going between meals.
     - **Stay hydrated**: Carry a refillable water bottle and use the free water refill stations around the parks.

4. **Stay Flexible with Your Schedule**
   - **Why It's Important**: While it's great to have a plan, Tokyo Disney Resort can be unpredictable—rides break down, weather changes, and some shows might be canceled. Staying flexible will allow you to adapt and enjoy the resort's offerings without stress.
   - **What to Do**: Be open to spontaneity and shift your plans based on **weather conditions**, **ride availability**, and

crowd levels. If one ride has a long line, try a different one and check back later.

5. **Utilize the App's Real-Time Updates**

    - **Why It's Important**: The Tokyo Disney Resort app is invaluable when it comes to staying on top of **real-time information**. From ride wait times to restaurant reservations, the app is your best tool for navigating the park.

    - **What to Do**: Check the app **frequently** throughout the day for updates on ride times, show schedules, dining availability, and special events. This will help you make the most of your time and avoid frustration.

Final Words of Inspiration

Tokyo Disney Resort is a place where dreams come true, and I want to leave you with a few **final words of inspiration** to help you fully embrace the magic that awaits you.

1. **Let Go of Perfection**

    - It's easy to get caught up in making everything perfect, but remember—your time at Tokyo Disney Resort is about **having fun** and **making memories**, not ticking off every item on a list. Embrace the unexpected moments, the spontaneous laughter, and the joy of simply being in the park.

2. **Be in the Moment**
   - Take time to enjoy the **small details** that make Disney special: the sparkle in your child's eyes when they meet their favorite character, the magical glow of **Cinderella Castle** at night, and the feeling of **wonder** as you embark on each adventure. These are the moments you'll remember long after your trip.

3. **Create Memories with Loved Ones**
   - Whether you're with family, friends, or even solo, Tokyo Disney Resort is about **shared experiences**. Laugh with your loved ones during the parades, cheer each other on during the rides, and create lasting memories that you'll treasure forever.

4. **Stay Open to the Magic**
   - Tokyo Disney Resort has a way of surprising you with magic when you least expect it. Whether it's a spontaneous **character meet-and-greet**, an **unexpected show** starting, or a beautiful **sunset over DisneySea**, always stay open to the surprises that await you. You never know what delightful experience might come your way.

Bonus Content

I'm excited to provide you with an exclusive **Packing List** to ensure you're fully prepared for your magical trip to Tokyo Disney Resort. Whether you're planning a short stay or an extended adventure, having the right items with you can make all the difference. From **weather-appropriate clothing** to **tech gear** for staying connected, this list will help you pack efficiently and confidently.

Packing List for Tokyo Disney Resort

Clothing

☐ Comfortable Walking Shoes (for lots of walking around the parks)

☐ Weather-Appropriate Apparel

☐ Summer: Lightweight clothing, hats, sunglasses, and sunscreen

☑ Winter: Layers, a warm jacket, gloves, and scarves

☐ Rain Gear (lightweight rain poncho or umbrella)

☐ Swimwear (if visiting pools or water attractions)

Tech Essentials

☐ Smartphone (with the Tokyo Disney Resort app installed)

☑ Portable Charger (for keeping your devices powered throughout the day)

☐ Camera (and waterproof case if planning to ride water attractions)

☐ Universal Adapter (for charging electronics, Japan uses type A and B plugs)

Health and Comfort

☐ Sunscreen (SPF 30 or higher)

☐ Prescription Medications (in original containers)

☐ Personal First-Aid Kit (band-aids, pain relievers, antiseptic wipes)

☐ Hand Sanitizer (for quick cleanliness on-the-go)

Documents

☐ Passport (required for international travel)

☐ Park Tickets and Reservations (print or save digital copies)

☐ Travel Insurance Information (ensure it covers health and cancellations)

Miscellaneous

☐ Reusable Water Bottle (refillable at water stations around the park)

☐ Snacks (granola bars, trail mix, etc. for quick energy boosts)

☐ Small Backpack or Bag (for carrying essentials while in the park)

☐ Ponchos or Ziplock Bags (for wet clothes or protecting electronics)

Before You Leave

☐ Book Flights (confirm dates and times, check-in online)

☐ Arrange Airport Transfers (to and from Tokyo Disney Resort)

☐ Double-Check Reservations (hotel, dining, FastPass)

☐ Currency Exchange (bring yen for small purchases)

☐ Prepare Travel Insurance (ensure it covers health, cancellations, and special needs)

Packing and Preparation

☐ Review the Weather Forecast (check for current Tokyo weather)

☐ Download Useful Apps (Tokyo Disney Resort app, Google Maps, translation apps)

☐ Download Itinerary and Maps (store in phone for quick reference)

On the Day of Departure

☐ Arrive Early at the Airport (for check-in and security)

☐ Pack Snacks and Entertainment for Travel (especially for long flights or train rides)

☐ Confirm Transportation to the Resort (ensure you know how to get from Tokyo Airport to your Disney hotel)

At Tokyo Disney Resort

☐ Arrive Early to the Park (to maximize your day and enjoy attractions without long waits)

☐ Make Dining and Show Reservations Early (using the Tokyo Disney Resort app)

☐ Take Breaks (find quiet spots to rest and hydrate during the day)

☐ Keep Track of Your Personal Belongings (store valuables securely in your bag)

Additional Tips and Tricks

☐ Use FastPasses for Popular Rides (for shorter wait times at high-demand attractions)

☐ Use Single Rider Lines (to bypass long queues if you're visiting solo or don't mind riding separately)

☐ Bring Snacks and Water (to keep your energy up without missing out on the fun)

☐ Stay Flexible (be open to changing your plans based on ride availability or weather conditions)

FAQs

1. **What are the park hours for Tokyo Disneyland and Tokyo DisneySea?**
   - Tokyo Disneyland and Tokyo DisneySea generally open around 8:00 AM and close around 9:00 PM, though hours can vary depending on the season, special events, and maintenance schedules. Always check the official website or the Tokyo Disney Resort app for the most up-to-date information before your visit.

2. **Can I buy tickets for Tokyo Disney Resort in advance?**
   - Yes, it's highly recommended to purchase your tickets in advance to guarantee entry, especially during peak seasons. Tickets can be purchased on the official Tokyo Disney Resort website, at official travel agents, or at the park gates (if available). Make sure to check for any online discounts or special offers before buying.

3. **Do I need to book a FastPass in advance?**
   - FastPasses are available on a first-come, first-served basis and can be obtained at the park on the day of your visit. However, there are options to reserve some rides through the Tokyo Disney Resort app, depending on the attraction

and current availability. It's advisable to use FastPasses early in the day for the most popular attractions to minimize wait times.

4. **What is the best time of year to visit Tokyo Disney Resort?**

    - The best time to visit depends on your preferences. If you prefer fewer crowds and better weather, consider visiting during the **spring** (March-May) or **autumn** (September-November). However, these seasons are also when special events and festivals occur, which can draw in larger crowds. If you want to experience Tokyo Disney Resort in its full festive glory, **Christmas** (November-December) and **Halloween** (September-October) are great times to visit.

5. **Is Tokyo Disney Resort accessible for people with disabilities?**

    - Yes, Tokyo Disney Resort offers various services and facilities for guests with disabilities. These include **Disability Access Services (DAS)**, which provide access to shorter wait times, wheelchair and ECV rentals, accessible restrooms, and more. The park is designed to be inclusive, and guests with special needs are encouraged to visit Guest Relations for assistance.

6. **Can I bring my own food into Tokyo Disney Resort?**
    - Outside food and beverages are generally not permitted inside Tokyo Disney Resort, with some exceptions for guests with dietary restrictions, allergies, or young children. However, you can bring small snacks like granola bars or fruit for quick energy boosts. It's best to check the specific guidelines on the official website before your visit.

7. **Are there any special dining experiences at Tokyo Disney Resort?**
    - Yes, Tokyo Disney Resort offers various **themed dining experiences**, such as character dining, buffet meals, and exclusive dining events. Some of the most popular options include **Character Dining at the Disneyland Hotel** and themed restaurants like **Queen of Hearts Banquet Hall** and **Café Orleans** in Disneyland. Reservations are highly recommended for these special experiences.

8. **What type of transportation options are available to get to Tokyo Disney Resort?**
    - Tokyo Disney Resort is accessible by train, bus, taxi, and private shuttle services. The closest train stations are **Maihama Station** and **Tokyo Disneyland Station**, which are directly

connected to both Tokyo Disneyland and Tokyo DisneySea. If you are staying at a Disney hotel, you can also use free shuttle services to the parks. Public buses also provide access to the resort from Tokyo city.

9. **Can I leave the park and come back the same day?**

    - Yes, you can exit and re-enter the park the same day if you have a valid ticket. However, you will need to get a re-entry pass when you leave the park. Make sure to check the park's re-entry policy, as it might vary depending on special events or busy periods.

10. **Is there a way to skip the long lines at Tokyo Disney Resort?**

    - The best way to skip long lines is to use the **FastPass** system for popular attractions, which allows you to reserve a time slot for certain rides. Additionally, you can use the **Tokyo Disney Resort app** to monitor real-time wait times and plan your day around the least crowded attractions.

11. **Are there any discounts for Tokyo Disney Resort tickets?**

    - Tokyo Disney Resort occasionally offers discounts for children, seniors, and multi-day tickets. Additionally, some local residents might have access to special promotions. It's also worth checking travel agencies, as they sometimes offer bundled deals that include tickets, hotel accommodations, and other services.

12. **What should I pack for my visit to Tokyo Disney Resort?**

    - You should pack comfortable shoes, sunscreen, a hat, and a rain poncho (in case of sudden rain showers). If you plan on taking photos, don't forget your camera or phone with plenty of battery life. A portable charger is also recommended for staying connected and using the Tokyo Disney Resort app.

13. **Are there any height restrictions for attractions?**

    - Yes, there are certain height restrictions for some rides at Tokyo Disney Resort, such as **Big Thunder Mountain**, **Space Mountain**, and **Splash Mountain**. Be sure to check the height requirements before getting in line, which are clearly displayed at each attraction.

14. **Can I meet Disney characters at Tokyo Disney Resort?**

    - Yes, character meet-and-greets are available throughout the park, including popular characters like **Mickey Mouse**, **Minnie Mouse**, **Goofy**, **Donald**

Duck, and others. You can find these meet-and-greet locations in the **Tokyo Disneyland** and **Tokyo DisneySea** areas, and it's advisable to check the schedules on the Tokyo Disney Resort app to find out where and when the characters will appear.

15. **Are there any seasonal events or parades at Tokyo Disney Resort?**
    - Yes, Tokyo Disney Resort celebrates a variety of seasonal events throughout the year, including **Halloween, Christmas**, and **New Year's**. These events feature special **parades, shows**, and **themed decorations**. Make sure to check the event calendar for the exact dates and details of these celebrations.

16. **What is the difference between Tokyo Disneyland and Tokyo DisneySea?**
    - **Tokyo Disneyland** is more traditional and features the classic Disney characters, themes, and attractions like **Pirates of the Caribbean, Splash Mountain**, and **It's a Small World**. **On** the other hand, Tokyo DisneySea is more unique and focuses on maritime themes, offering attractions like **Journey to the Center of the Earth** and **Tower of Terror**. Both parks offer distinct experiences and are worth visiting during your trip.

17. **What is the best way to get around the parks?**

    - Walking is the best way to get around Tokyo Disney Resort, as both parks are relatively compact. However, suppose you need to travel between Tokyo Disneyland and Tokyo DisneySea. In that case, you can take the complimentary Disney Resort Line monorail, which has convenient stops at key locations in both parks and hotels.

18. **Are there any exclusive experiences at Tokyo Disney Resort?**

    - Tokyo Disney Resort offers **exclusive experiences** such as VIP tours, private events, and behind-the-scenes tours. These options can be customized to include personal guides, reserved seating for parades and shows, and special access to attractions. Be sure to book these experiences in advance, as they are limited in availability.

19. **What is the Tokyo Disney Resort app, and how can it help?**

    - The **Tokyo Disney Resort app** is an essential tool for navigating the parks. It provides real-time information about **ride wait times**, **show schedules**, **restaurant menus**, and **dining reservations**. You can also use the app to book FastPasses, check park hours, and find the best routes to attractions. It's a must-have for maximizing your time in the parks.

20. **Can I buy Disney merchandise outside the parks?**

    - Tokyo Disney Resort offers **official Disney merchandise** in various locations around Tokyo, including select shopping malls and department stores. You can also find unique items in **airport shops** before you leave Japan.

21. **What kind of food is available at Tokyo Disney Resort?**

    - Tokyo Disney Resort offers a wide variety of **themed dining experiences**, from quick-service restaurants to fine dining. Popular options include **character dining**, **buffets**, and **themed eateries** like **Queen of Hearts Banquet Hall** and **Café Orleans**. You'll find an array of **international and Japanese cuisine**, including sushi, ramen, and Mickey-shaped snacks.

22. **Are there any accommodations near Tokyo Disney Resort?**

    - Yes, there are severalseveral **Disney-themed hotels** located right next to the resort, such as **Disneyland Hotel**, **Tokyo DisneySea Hotel MiraCosta**, and **Disney's Ambassador Hotel**. These hotels offer exclusive benefits such as early park entry and convenient park access. Additionally, many off-site hotels are within walking distance or a short monorail ride from the resort.

23. **Can I visit both Tokyo Disneyland and Tokyo DisneySea in one day?**

    - It's possible to visit both parks in one day, but spending at least one full day at each park is highly recommended. Tokyo Disney Resort offers a **Park Hopper Ticket**, allowing you to visit both parks on the same day. However, to fully enjoy the attractions and shows at both parks, you must plan your visit carefully and arrive early.

24. **Are there any unique experiences you can only find at Tokyo Disney Resort?**

    - Tokyo Disney Resort offers some unique experiences that you won't find at other Disney parks, such as **Pirates of the Caribbean** in Tokyo Disneyland (which is different from other parks' versions) and the **Tower of Terror** ride at DisneySea, which has an entirely different storyline. The park's dedication to detail and beautiful design is also unique, especially in **DisneySea**, which has more mature, unique themes than other Disney parks.

Photo section

TOKYO DISNEYSEA HOTEL

PIRATES OF THE CARRIBEAN

BIG THUNDER MOUNTAIN

189 |TOKYO DISNEY RESORT

POOH'S HUNNY HUNT

PLAZA GARDENS RESTAURANT

CHEF MICKEY'S RESTAURANT

THE LITTLE MERMAID RIDE

THE LITTLE MERMAID RIDE

Made in the USA
Coppell, TX
05 May 2025

49015018R00108